D1420719

# Attention to Detail

Suzanne Trocmé

# Attention to Detail

Photography by Andrew Wood

CREATING CONTEMPORARY HOMES

Jacqui Small

*To Catherine Rubinstein, with thanks*

First published in 2004 by Jacqui Small,
an imprint of Aurum Press Ltd,
25 Bedford Avenue, London WC1B 3AT



Publisher Jacqui Small
Editor Catherine Rubinstein
Designer Lawrence Morton
Location Researcher Nadine Bazar
Floorplans Jan Douglas
Production Geoff Barlow

A catalogue record for this book is available from the British Library.

ISBN 1 903221 22 6

2006 2005

10 9 8 7 6 5 4 3 2

Printed in Hong Kong

# CONTENTS

**Introduction 6**

**Casebook 12**
Living Room 14
Dining Room 34
Kitchen 44
Connecting Space 56
Bedroom 68
Bathroom 78

**Functional Detail 96**
Surfaces 98
  Walls 100
  Floors 114
Structure 124
Services 142
  Water 144
  Heat 154
  Light 162
Storage 172

**Decorative Detail 184**
Accessories 186
  Furniture 188
  Soft Furnishings 198
  Art & Ornament 206

Directory 212
Index 221
Acknowledgements 224

ALVAR AALTO
ALVAR AALTO
ALVAR AALTO
Les arts décoratifs de 1790 à 1850
L'architecture au XIXe siècle
CHINESE CERAMICS
NEW FORMS
Colours
CHAREAU
FRANK LLOYD WRIGHT
IN THE ORIENTAL STYLE
The Georgian House
Moroccan Interiors
London Interiors
outdoor living
IRISH
INDIAN STYLE
Indian Interiors
IDEAL CITIES
Islam Art and Architecture
ARNE JACOBSEN
ALEXANDRE NOLL
ROBERT COUTURIER
JEAN ROYÈRE
MAXIME OLD
ANDRÉ ARBUS
LES FRÈRES PERRET
RAPHAEL
GIO PONTI
WHAT MODERN WAS
MODERN FURNITURE CLASSICS
STYLES
TASCHEN

# INTRODUCTION

Each morning I leave my London home by taxi, and traverse two bridges over the same river, a U-shaped journey, to reach my office. On a good day it takes six minutes. Lambeth Bridge takes me to the south bank of the Thames and, having travelled along the river's edge, I return to the other side via Waterloo Bridge. The bend in the river means the journey is not as long as it sounds, but the predominant reason for this route is that Waterloo Bridge happens to be one of my favourite works of architecture and I am fortunate enough to work at the top end of it. The bridge is an unpopular choice for aesthetes, since it is plain and functional, relatively unembellished – some people say that of my home too. But it possesses the best views in London, as well as hidden depths and an extraordinary history (it was rebuilt during World War II by women, who made the extravagant decision to use Portland stone, on the practical basis that it is self-cleaning and would remain a remarkable sight, echoing the stone of nearby St Paul's cathedral, white against the grey British skyline). So it is with a good home. How else do we choose our home's location (whether building or buying) except by vista and view, convenience for facilities and the security it brings?

Most people need to have a sense of place and, to a certain degree, routine, in and outside of the home. We are often drawn to live near water, and usually follow the same paths when journeying. Man has always sought order in the world and our homes are our base camps; they have become the nucleus around which we orbit and must remain secure on many levels, built well and to function as our supporting cast. It is detail that holds the key, not in terms of frippery and finery but through scrutiny of specifics in every aspect, from location and foundations onward. If well informed, we choose and shape our homes to reflect our lifestyles, ease our movement and bring solace when all else seems out of control. Since most of us do leave home to work, it seems appropriate to keep a home that is pleasant to return to in the evening, and since our minds tend to be cluttered with information by the end of a day, I believe the simpler the home the better. It must also be comfortable – but with attention given to detail, this may mean fewer cushions and more thought, for example, before deciding the width of a staircase; interior design and architecture, like music, are as much about mathematics as they are about mood.

Once location is resolved, we can consider the structure, materials and configuration of a home. Much depends on personal circumstances and priorities, practical as much as visionary: for some occupants the airy freedom of glass walls may be a prime attraction, or the flow of space resulting from open-plan living facilitated by modern reinforced frames; for others a degree of privacy is more important, even in a secluded rural location. A home for just one or two adults may work best on an open-plan basis, while one with children has greater need for separate rooms, and a house that is lived in twenty-four hours a day, seven days a week, may need multifunctional areas for different times of day. Whatever the configuration, we need to be able to circulate, moving freely between different tasks, pausing comfortably in areas of relaxation.

An extreme example of differing priorities is to be found in Mies van der Rohe's Farnsworth House (see also page 99), perched on columns in grassy meadow on a riverbank near Chicago. Although the trees, grass, and river are visible through the "walls" of the glass-box house, they seem, from inside it, distant and abstracted, as if forming a landscape painting. When we scrutinise the interior of the house, however, there is no denying the sense of exposure: the interior is one large room subdivided by a free-standing wooden core, which encloses two bathrooms, a galley kitchen and a fireplace; the living areas are open and unbounded, the objects within seem tangible and tactile, and sights and sounds are magnified. The architecture calls not only to itself, but to the physical and esthetic experience of its occupant. Mies, in his mind, was successful in his mission. The occupant of the house, in contrast, was utterly uncomfortable with such an exhibitionist way of living: without doubt, it was the wrong home for this particular personality.

If renovating rather than building afresh, the options are generally restricted by what already exists, but this can lead to interesting results. In an acclaimed East Anglian barn conversion by Anthony Hudson, for instance, the walls of straw bale – not a material that would have been chosen if building today – allowed the creation of unusual detail, with a window wall on the sunny south-facing side and small slitlike windows on the sunless northern side. Similarly, restoration of Pam Skaist Levy's Hollywood Hills home has been largely shaped by the decision to retain the house's original post-and-beam construction and stained-glass panels. Reconfiguration can be dramatically effective, as evidenced by John Stedila's Long Island former fire station that has been opened up into an airy weekend escape for a single inhabitant, or by Jasper Conran's huge London living room that was a ballroom in its previous incarnation.

With each space or room's purpose set, the bare bones, service infrastructure (plumbing, wiring, heating, light, storage) and other functional details must be considered: what will be most efficient and practical, as well as looking good. remember not to confuse detail with decoration. Surfaces – floors, walls and furniture – are particularly crucial in setting the tone, especially in a contemporary home. The trend is generally, but not exclusively, toward simplicity; however, the apparent epitome of simplicity may not be as simple as it seems. The marble walls of a bathroom in a chic district of Brussels by Belgian architect Vincent Van Duysen, for instance, may appear to be just plain white marble but, like Waterloo Bridge, they are the result of a great deal of thought and co-operative effort from many people, with strict constraints on mining to avoid veined stone.

Finally come the decorative details – furniture, soft furnishings, window treatments, art and ornament. Design professionals have the responsibility to continue the thought process and the consideration for detail through both more and less technical aspects of each room, and must aim to provide the end user with a faultless facility.

Many architects and designers today tend to believe in simplicity, but there can still be an interesting role for decorative detail, in new and modern forms. As the late great Milanese architect Renzo Mongiardino (who died in 1998) put it, "Intelligent use of materials stems from a love of those materials and also from a knowledge of ways in which to exploit them most effectively, with the understanding that, when the appropriate material is not available, it may be simulated." Mongiardino, a master of decorative detail and creator of atmospheric "roomscapes", also pointed out the value of illusion: "Illusion comes into being as part of the pleasure of working on a surface, using more or less precious materials – stone, terracotta, wood, marble, fabric, leather, to imitate a new architecture."

Over time, details change. Not only do new materials and technologies become available for everyday use, thereby opening new possibilities in interior design, but each decade tends to bring its own lifestyle, and the result is changing identities and new problems with new solutions. As Horace said in his *Odes*, "Nothing is an unmixed blessing." We are today witnessing a move toward hidden facilities, such as underfloor heating (of course conceived by the Romans), wireless sound and flexless lighting. Some of us already have WIFI: even e-mail and Internet communication can be wireless. Imperfections in a modern home are more noticeable than in previous eras since we have stripped the home almost bare, so we notice indiscretions more and, moreover, have higher standards than before. Ironically, in creating a smoothly contemporary home, we are attempting, in a sense, to take the mechanics out of the "machine for living in", a perspective on homes discussed by the legendary architect Le Corbusier in his seminal work *Vers une architecture* in 1923.

*Attention to Detail* embraces different modern tastes as well as technological advancement, and is intended as a journey, an epic voyage in the manner of Cervantes via both magnitude and microcosm, through homes in many parts of Europe and America. Detail, as opposed to detailing, begins with the fundamentals, with foundation, and ends with the minutiae that assist in further personalising a home. Just as the better forms of education are designed to help students in their own development of ideas, this book has been written in the hope that its readers will take the information here as a starting point for their own ideas, which will undoubtedly mutate into better, or at least more fitting, solutions for their own very personal homes. The creation of a home is also a journey, with a beginning, a middle and an end, and countless memories of beyond.

Houses have history and soul, even if relatively newly built, since the mere construction of a house can take time, imagination and emotional effort. Whether building from the ground up or just restoring or creating a better interior environment in which to live, it is always the attention given to the detail and the thought process behind the building, the practical decisions, the problems solved, that will make one home seem more remarkable over another, just as Waterloo Bridge is more remarkable on many levels than other bridges on the Thames.

# CASEBOOK

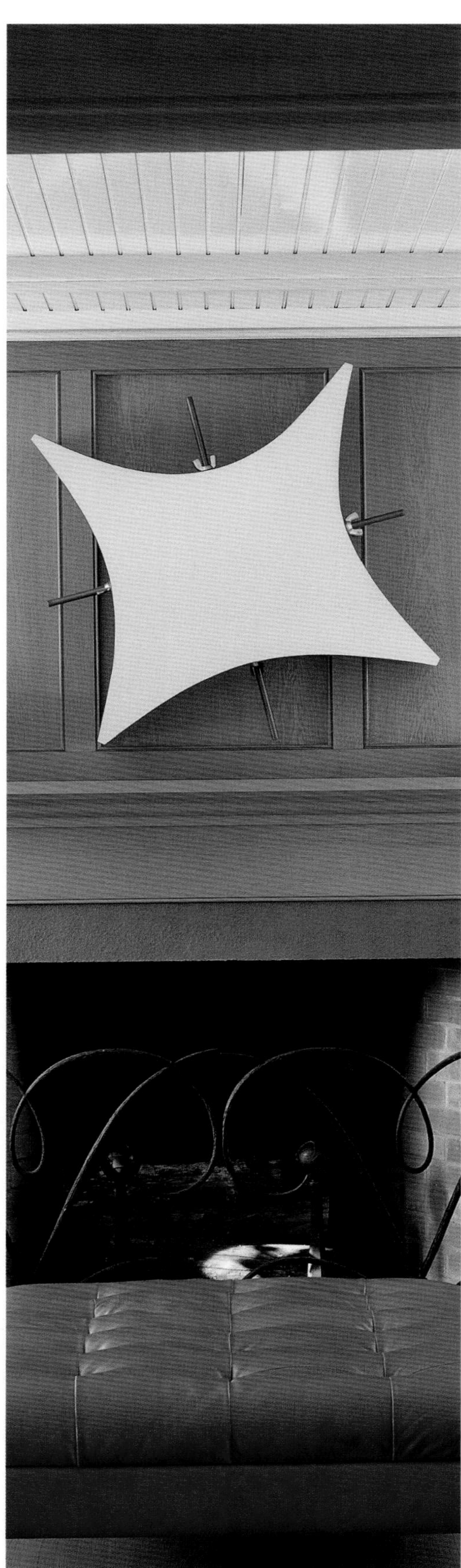

CHINESE CERAMICS
Islam
Art and Architecture
IDEAL CITIES
ARNE JACOBSEN
GIO PONTI
STYLES

# in the living room

In Roman times, Cicero, orator and politician, recommended remembering a lengthy and complex speech by imagining it as a journey through a building with, at particular locations, objects that would remind the speaker of the next succinct point to be made. By mentally visiting each in turn, orators could find their way through a long train of thought without written prompts. This is a very useful tool for remembering speeches. Perhaps when considering a home we should construct a similar plan, where key objects or elements , in other words the detailing of the fabrication of the home at junctures along the way, trigger more complex ideas. This kind of deliberation leads to memorable housing well worthy of discussion, as are the case studies in this chapter.

The living room marks the beginning of the journey through a home: it is the first room we consider when buying a house, no matter whether we are immediately on entry plunged into it or enter via a hallway. Thus details of a living room, aesthetic and practical, should contain succinct pointers to the tone of the rest of the home.

In the Western world at least, today's living room is usually multifunctional, used for many aspects of living; it was born from an amalgam of the salon, parlour and, often, dining room (many of us dine informally in the kitchen and more formally in the living room, space being at a premium today). For apartments, open-plan living is still in vogue, while the prime alternative is a central or main room, usually the living room, with cells of rooms leading from it. In modern houses, and I mean modern with a small m, when there is more than a single storey, each floor tends to contain a main room – downstairs the living room, upstairs generally the principal bedroom suite – which not only anchors that floor but sets its aesthetic theme.

Of course, we generally advocate the visual whole continuing from floor to floor, which can be achieved through colour palette or another kind of holding pattern, but change in function from room to room often means alternative materials are required for comfort and practical purposes. Nonetheless, these can be linked visually in many ways: consideration for detail in the living room, whether evoking seamlessness or syncopation, sets the tone for the rest of the home. From this central core, the attention to detail must continue from room to room, even with slight differences, through hallways and passageways, so that transversing one room to another is a pleasing and memorable experience.

In practical terms, the living room requires, above all, comfort, which begins with planning what is to be achieved in the space. Challenges in any room include heating it properly, lighting it adequately, ensuring that no obtrusive cables are visible, and creating levels out of larger and open-plan spaces so that the fluid whole of the architecture is not disrupted. These challenges are all the greater in a multifunctional living area. Saving space by utilising it well is a prime concern. Radiators and cables take up space, and technology is preparing the way for invisibility of such basics. With today's high standards, creating a fine contemporary living space can require more knowledge of detail than restoring a historical room.

CASE STUDY | 1

**comfort** *Ralph and Ann Pucci's house in Bedford, New York, has the luxury of three rooms for living (plus a dining room): a main room for reading and relaxing, a more diminutive "snug" cum library, and a vast family room next to the kitchen. The principal room in particular combines precision and comfort.*

***This picture*** The designer Wolf's signature pieces include overscale furniture and slipcovered or simply upholstered chairs; he has a penchant for eliminating skirting boards, mouldings and other contractor detailing that detract from a "clean" space. Oversized cushions add further comfort and drama.

***Above*** One of the shorter walls of the sepia-toned room hosts a Bettina Werner painting above an Art Nouveau iron table. The upholstered wooden bench seat is by Vicente Wolf for Niedermaier.

***Above right*** Tables are positioned alongside chairs for comfort, yet act as pretty tablescapes of highly edited objects. The tension between traditional and modern and the casual combination of style and periods in a pristine environment ensure an enduring timelessness.

**In the quest for perfection,** design expert Ralph Pucci commissioned interior designer Vicente Wolf to assist with his home, a grey-shingled dwelling. Wolf understood that the Puccis, who grew up in close proximity to each other and married young, had similar taste, that they liked their environment to be "neat but easy". For their voluminous Westchester County home, Wolf decided to pay attention to comfort and materials.

His approach was that every element must seem to be "destined" rather than "simply arranged". The materials – wood, limestone (the fireplace), linen, velvet and worn leather – became prominent features in the room, and the coffee and cream tones assist in keeping the potential noise of a heavily furnished room, figuratively speaking, to a pitch

CLEMENTE

**A** Entry steps down
**B** Long sofa
**C** Built-in bookshelves
**D** New windows
**E** Stone fireplace
**F** Bay window
**G** Curved sofa
**H** Bleached-wood floor
**I** Carpet

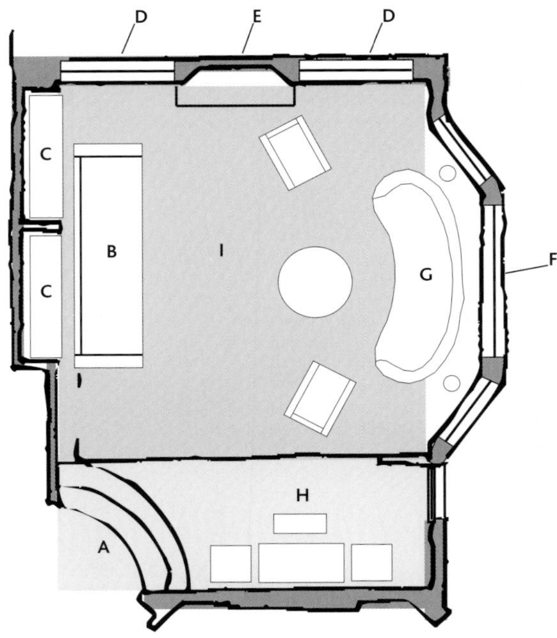


barely audible. Three main islands of furniture, from many sources, can be regrouped for different occupants. A bay window takes up one long wall, opposite a bookshelf unit with luxurious seating in front. At one end of the room, a still-life grouping echoes the symmetry of the fireplace wall at the other end.

Light from the garden to the living room flows through Roman shades made from translucent linen, its quality allowing the inside and outside to remain linked. The scrim allies the windows with the walls. The clarity of the rest of the house exudes from the living room, for which furniture has been created as if couture.

A journey around this room indicates that its balance of textures and forms, and the consequent success of the interior landscape – despite inclusion of numerous objects and pieces of furniture – is more a result of contouring than of decorating. Scale has been carefully considered: the massive, plump sofas can accommodate the largest of guests, yet possess an element of demureness due to their height and the selection of a simple but robust quality of upholstery fabric. The small tables are placed wherever they have real use, by armchairs and in front of sofas for books and drinks. The luxuriousness of the carpet adds to the luscious quality of a room that is at once relaxing and functional.

***Above left*** The step down to the living room from the entrance hall is marked by an alteration in flooring materials. Surfaces and contrast play an important role in the house: most walls are pure white and floors are dark wood or bleached.

***Right*** Upholstery is understated beige linen, cured-tobacco limousine cloth or tweedy brown chenille. The deep dish sofa is by Vicente Wolf; the table with granite top and gilded curved legs is vintage French 1940s, the other of similar materials but pure Wolf style.

CHÂTEAUX OF THE LOIRE
Provence Interiors
NAPOLEON
ART AT WORK
Biedermeier
HENRI MATISSE
A RETROSPECTIVE
JOAN MITCHELL PASTEL
MOTHERWELL
New York Interiors
APPEARANCES
FRAGONARD
Picasso and Portraiture
UNSEEN WARHOL
GAVINA
AMERICAN ART DECO
ISSEY MIYAKE East Meets West
CANOVA
Jackson Pollock
BRANCUSI
GIORGIO ARMANI
MODERN FURNITURE CLASSICS
AMERICAN
PAST PRESENT François-Marie BANIER

***This page*** The lofty living space has seating as deep as a bed, its feet of mirrored glass echoing other glistening elements in the home including the poured resin floor, which contains mother-of-pearl for added sparkle. Beyond the low wooden table by Habitat is the dining area.

***Opposite*** The domed light fixture above the informal dining table has a refined and uneven form, is paper-thin although produced from composite, and acts as sculpture, distracting from its utilitarian purpose. It was designed by Colleoni.

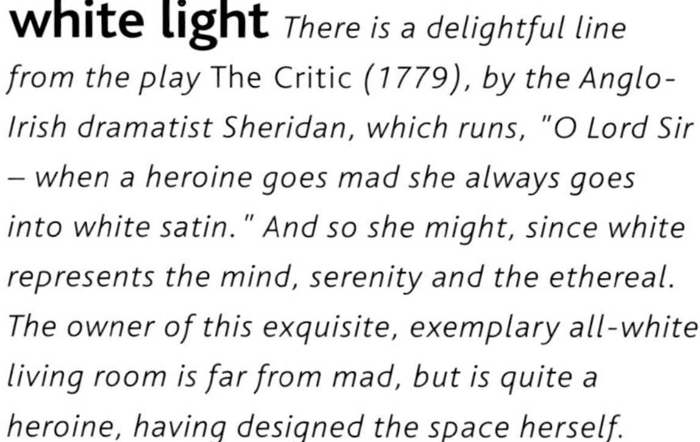

CASE STUDY | 2

## white light

*There is a delightful line from the play* The Critic *(1779), by the Anglo-Irish dramatist Sheridan, which runs, "O Lord Sir – when a heroine goes mad she always goes into white satin." And so she might, since white represents the mind, serenity and the ethereal. The owner of this exquisite, exemplary all-white living room is far from mad, but is quite a heroine, having designed the space herself.*

***Above*** Flat-faced supporting columns (there are two in the living area) cleverly conceal the spotlighting, way above head height, to eliminate any disturbance from obtrusive fixtures.

**Susanna Colleoni, the Italian head** of PR for the fashion house Missoni, bought her two-storey courtyarded pavilion, at the rear of an older property in Milan, from an architect who had used it as his office. The only remnants of that period are the massive double-height bookcases at alternate ends of opposing walls in the open-plan loft-style living space that takes up the majority of the dwelling.

Since the previous owner's day, the space has been resurfaced and redesigned; the whole living area is now white, maximising space and light. Walls are painted builder's white, and the floor is a white resin which appears slightly pinkish, due to crushed mother-of-pearl that was mixed into the resin before pouring, effectively giving it a look of effervescent champagne. These whites are a contrast to the jazzy patterns and colours of Missoni with which Colleoni has worked for fifteen years. "The light colours are harmonising and a perfect antidote to the greyness of the city. And for me, white and cream are synonymous with harmony and freedom," she explains.

The home now is an expert lesson in the use of materials to maximise light. Full-height pivoting glass doors link the living area to the kitchen, and more glass doors lead from the kitchen to the bedroom wing. Apart from the ultra-tall bookcases, the sleek furniture is under waist height, to bring out the feeling of spaciousness.

Unlike most Italian homes, it has no entrance hall; entry is directly into the living room, which is shielded by a large freestanding closet for coats. To the right, an informal dining area sits underneath a domed light fixture, and a seating area with a minimal fireplace is just beyond. The formal dining area is strict in its simplicity: fabric used for upholstery is shiny to reflect light, the entire space an experiment in surface texture and play of light.

Yet this is far from a whitewashed home. Every element has been created with as much care and attention as some designers give to the restoration of a palazzo. Its unity is its rich whiteness, its contrast in its materials. The whites appear different since light is absorbed and reflected differently according to the surface used. Throughout, Colleoni's home reflects her love for modern materials.

***Right*** Two bookcases remain from the previous owner, although now painted white. Their square forms make for two very graphic anchors to the space, which seems almost held rigid by their tautness. The living room is furnished with pieces by the Italian Cyrus company, including the pendant lamp, table, sofas and poufs.

***Below*** The minimal fireplace is simply cut out of a new "floating" wall, reminiscent of the Modernist architecture favoured by the owner.

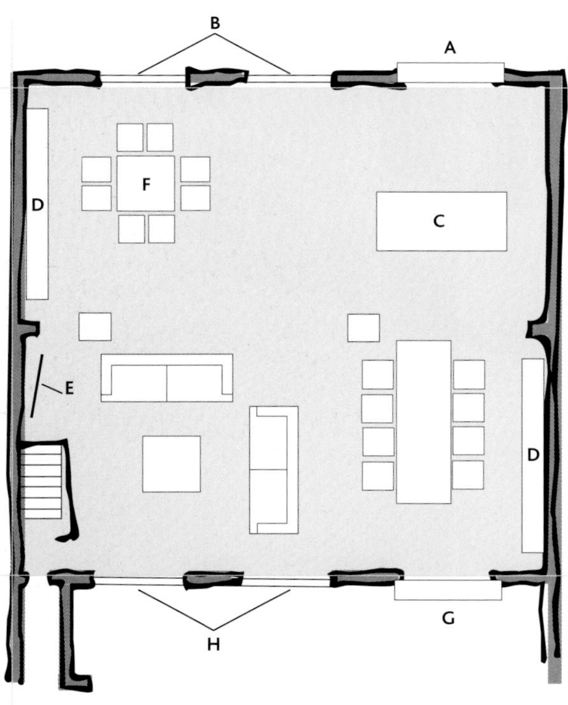


**A** Door from outer courtyard
**B** Windows to outer courtyard
**C** Closet
**D** Bookcases
**E** New fireplace in floating wall
**F** Low table and seating
**G** Pivoting glass doors
**H** Windows to inner courtyard

**texture** *A large, ambitious country home in upstate New York was tackled by city architecture firm Shelton, Mindel & Associates with all the application and spectacular talent they had brought to the same clients' Manhattan townhouse. The owners – a vibrant, successful young couple – approached the project like landscape designers of centuries gone by.*

***This picture*** The L-shaped sofa in chocolate epinglé fabric was designed and produced by Shelton, Mindel & Associates for the project. The two small rare tables are *c.* 1955 by George Nakashima, the Nigerian leather chair a museum-quality piece by Danish designer Kaare Klint. The lamp, one of a pair, is French Arts and Crafts.

***Right*** German white rift oak is omnipresent in this home, selected for appropriate graining, or lack of it. Other accents of wood, here an accessory added later, contribute to the complex but natural colour palette.

**The Rhinebeck "farm"** consisted of five separate large wooden buildings, including two houses, a short walk away from one another, situated in over forty hectares (one hundred acres). The clients have since purchased about the same again, as far as the eye can see. Hundreds of tons of landfill have been brought in to create a rolling landscape rivalled only, centuries ago, by Capability Brown; with great perception, the lady of the house insists that the landscape they have created should not be diminished by the prospect of developers in what remains unspoiled territory.

The couple selected Shelton and Mindel because, paradoxically, of the way the architects approach urban space. The firm's philosophy is tripartite, from the genesis of

***Left*** This sofa, in raw goldenish linen, is quite a country cousin. The pair of chairs in original brown leather are Fritz Henningsen from 1927. The blown-glass apple, on an octagonal Arts and Crafts table, is from the Swedish company Orrefors.

***Right*** The fire surround is German white rift oak and grey slate, with a sinuous shield of hand-forged iron. In front, the button-topped ottoman in tan leather was custom-made (it is hard to find "comfort" furniture to fit such a tailored scheme). The art above the fireplace is by designer Brad Dunning.

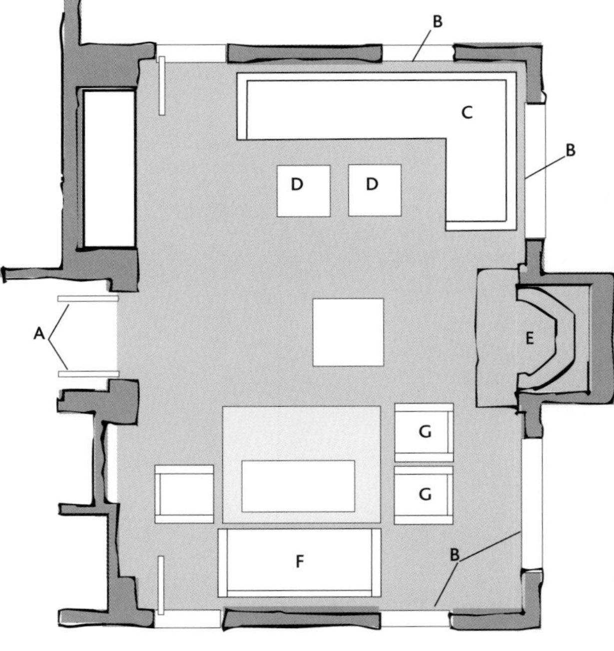


**A** Oak doors
**B** Linen and voile curtains
**C** Dark-brown L-shaped sofa
**D** Nakashima tables
**E** Oak and slate fireplace
**F** Golden linen-covered sofa
**G** Henningsen chairs

the project, when information is gathered and assimilated, through "architectonics", when the rules of design are built to protect the integrity of the concept, and finally to the interpretation. The main house, which has become the family's second home, is at once picturesque and handsome: a large rectangular two-storey, pitched-roof building with a legion of windows along both long sides.

Fully symmetrical, the living room is reached from the end of a corridor, through German oak double doors; it spans from side to side of the shorter end of the house, thus possessing a triple aspect – three windowed exterior walls, the room awash with filtered sunlight. The room appears suspended near the ceiling from hand-forged bronze curtain poles, and contained within ecru linen and voile curtains "the colour of the light", according to Mindel. Designed to be fully used, this room can comfortably seat a dozen people. Chair backs throughout the house allow for a gentle arm rest, a pivot on which to move to accommodate conversation. Plump cushions give further reassurance.

All rooms on the ground floor have elements of oak cladding (see pages 106–7). The lady of the house dedicated significant time to selecting not just the perfect graining of timber but the actual trees that would be felled. This is a home of dedication, of substance, yet made to look oh so simple – and preciousness has no place: "The children and dogs climb everywhere," she says.

CASE STUDY | 4

## colour *Bold, rich use of colour can add a touch of voluptuousness to an interior, particularly if it is in a dramatic and imposing, but relatively dark, Art Deco apartment building on New York's Upper West Side. Cocooning in winter, cooling in summer, this is a veritable home for all seasons.*

**A sludge colour palette** would have been the most unremarkable selection for this apartment. Although American Art Deco schemes seem, in retrospect, to have been quite glamorous, thanks to the Hollywood celluloid interpretation of the period – all glitzy black marble and glass – I am afraid as an Englishwoman I shy away from our interpretation of Deco, which was very much a poorer cousin based upon the Odeon style, and which unfortunately manifested itself into the mainstream in wartime and postwar British housing as a dirge of cinnamons, browns and dirty creams.

What interior designer John Barman has achieved here is a uplifting nod to the Art Deco period and a little beyond (there are a few 1940s and 1950s pieces) by concentrating on the forms of the furniture – square, low and

***Top*** On entry, the new curving staircase that unites the duplex levels catches the eye. The blue underneath sets the pace for the colour scheme, with the curved glass an inspired touch. The table is from the 1960s.

***Above*** Most walls were removed to allow light in, with remaining walls painted white. The jewel colour palette was inspired by the American figurative paintings hung throughout the living space.

***This picture*** The principal seating arrangement includes original Art Deco pieces upholstered in quality pile and cut-pile fabrics. Barman defined the different spaces within the room by strategically placing ultra-large rugs in contrasting colours. The windows overlook Central Park.

plump – and the fabrics (mainly piled, some even cut-pile and self-patterned), blended into a completely modernised look by injecting poster-paint reds and blues and, for a little lift, exotics such as lime green. Not for the faint-hearted, the scheme is at once elegant and cheery, as well as projecting the ultimate in comfort.

The initial part of the reconstruction of this interior was controlled by the clients' choice of architect, Alexander Gorlin, who unified the two floors with the dramatic spiral staircase and removed walls to bring light in and reapportion the space. Then John Barman and associate Kelly Graham produced the furnishings and interior concept. While the upper floor contains bedrooms and bathrooms, the ground floor appears open-plan – although there are in fact two small studies and a kitchen on this level. The open-plan living space, a successful area which can hold many people, has sections for different activities: one portion accommodates a piano, another section is partitioned off by a waist-height wall to contain a library and reading area.

Barman's design works because his choice of colour palette is as much a statement as the building itself. So often we witness a home owner adding black-and-white minimal furniture to a space that actually has period character; much better to go with the flow and add a little, in the most modern manner of course, rather than lose the character.

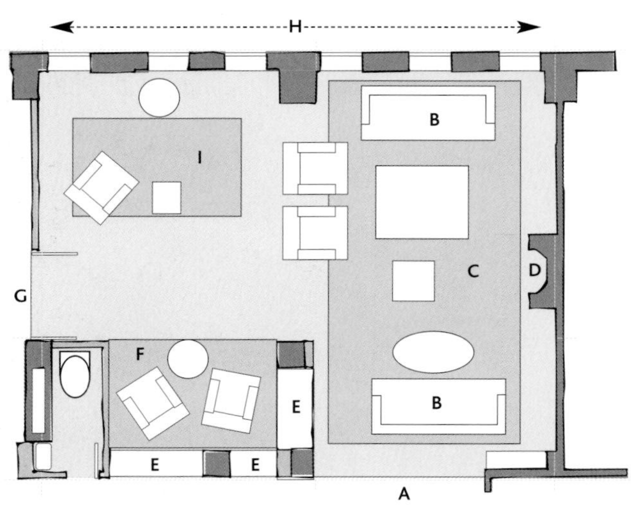


**A** Doorless entry from hallway and staircase
**B** Sofas
**C** Brown-and-ivory rug
**D** Stylised stone fireplace
**E** Waist-height shelves
**F** Library section, with red rug
**G** Entry to study
**H** Bank of windows
**I** Champagne rug

***Right*** Furniture was sourced around the world. A metal-based table with concave glass top by Gio Ponti from the 1950s finds its place on a shaggy red rug. Every decorative element has been carefully selected for what it might bring to the bold interior. The concave glass top is extremely deep.

***Far right, top*** The red rug portions off the library area, where shelving units are beneath waist height so as not to disturb the sight line throughout the main living area. Brown upholstered chairs are a sophisticated addition to the scheme.

***Far right, bottom*** The champagne shade of the rug, its pile cut to produce a dot-matrix pattern, harmonises with the chocolate-brown-and-ivory geometrically patterned rug nearby. Both carpets create spaces within a space. Using a lighter rug near the window lightened what was a dark space. Orange and red glass blown by the owners' teenage son (on a fine 1940s table) forms part of a colourful collection that includes cobalt-blue pieces by Elsa Peretti for Tiffany.

CASE STUDY | 5

**geometry** *Paris-based Eric Gizard designed his first London house, for a well-travelled French art collector and her English husband, in an unforgiving Notting Hill square. The five-storey white-fronted building epitomises his fascination with geometric opposition of rhythms and the role of light and shade.*

**A** Entry from landing
**B** Windows
**C** Re-edition "Barcelona" chairs
**D** Original fire mantel
**E** Sofas
**F** Rugs
**G** Double folding doors
**H** Low fireplace
**I** Bookcases

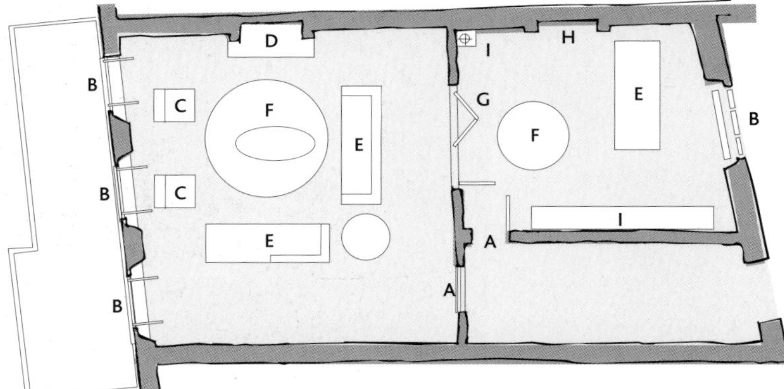


**Good design, I believe,** is movement that has come to rest. This house is exactly that, a fine example of balance and harmony, despite its clash of traditions – an English house with ostensibly modern French decor and world-friendly art. Gizard opened up all rooms, creating a front-to-back axis, daylight streaming through from the garden square in front and the rear garden. The interior was reconfigured and an extension added linking the lower two floors to the garden, which in effect became a mezzanine.

The double-aspect living rooms are on the floor above the ground floor; in a grand London house this was traditionally the elegant part. Internal doors have been opened up, and both rooms have a sense of geometry: one is more formal, retaining traditional architectural elements, carefully blended, while in the other entire walls have a painterly quality and textural differences bring the space to life. Fireplaces have remained, but have been simplified, made boxy. The result is warm yet contemporary.

***This picture*** To unify the two rooms the designer created a geometric wall whose fireplaces echo the abstract art in the front room and the metallic bookcase facade in the rear room. Sofas throughout were designed by Gizard for Paris Rive Gauche (Edition D'Argentat).

***Left*** The forms of furniture have been presented as "architecture in miniature" – sofas can be walked around as if buildings, with enough space to breathe. Elements such as the dados remain, but tie in well with the neoclassicism of the fireplace mantel.

# in the dining room

An awful lot can occur in a dining room. Over meals many great decisions have been made, and some terrible habits, including bad marriages, broken or eased, as Alfred, Lord Tennyson described in 1855: "You'll have no scandal while you dine, But honest talk and wholesome wine." So it is important when designing a home to linger hard on the details of a dining room, on its poetry beyond all else, but also on practicalities – relative height of table and chairs; ease of listening, i.e. sound absorption; whether a buffet or credenza will add or detract. If such details are wrong, diners do not linger and decisions are not made.

The dining room may be the place where most conscious time is spent. Time in the bedroom is mainly unconscious, in the living room often "semi" conscious, particularly if a television is involved. Unfortunately today we are often too hurried to enjoy dining, which has led to a glut of, well, gluttons, who gobble and run without thought for the food they have just consumed or the room they have dined in – a habit that should, in my opinion, be addressed.

I was fortunate enough to spend a considerable amount of time (a marriage) in France, in Paris and a nearby suburb, where I learned much about food and dining. First, I learned to shop daily at the local market. Supermarkets for me now mean utility goods, cleaning equipment and dried goods. All other comestibles come fresh to the mind and palate alike.

The second inspiration came from witnessing French women, most weighing in at around 110 pounds, tucking in to a two- if not three-course meal at every lunchtime opportunity, the trick being that the French tend not to eat between meals, lunch at noon, eat bread without butter, and drink red wine for "digestion". The lingering over lunch appealed most.

My sons' nursery school instigated the next surprise: a menu was pasted to the school gates each morning describing the lunch menu – always an appetiser, a main course, followed by a cheese course (the cheese was described) and an elaborate pudding. French children therefore know how to enjoy a lingering meal and eat with ceramic, glass and real knives and forks from a young age. Consequently, they – and mine, I proudly add – know how to behave in restaurants, are not afraid to experiment, and enjoy the eating experience. (Admittedly, polite conversation comes later, political discourse later still.) Perhaps this is why the French produce good dining rooms, on the whole. The Romans also understood the link between happiness and eating, Virgil pronouncing in his *Ecologues*, "*Incipe, parve puer: qui non risere parenti, Nec deus hunc mensa, dea nec dignata cunili est,*" which translates as "Begin, baby boy: if you haven't a smile for your parent, then neither will a god think you worth inviting to dinner, nor a goddess to bed." I'll explain the latter to my sons in time.

The whole experience of dining is important, and that in part comes from the room, tables, chairs and hardware, very much the supporting cast, without which the lead would falter. Clarity of vision on the design front cannot fail to give clarity of thought. None of the following dining rooms is in France, but these case studies prove that the art of dining can be successful in any modern home, if well thought out.

***This picture*** Coordinating dining-room equipment is concealed behind sliding doors which move from the top. Flooring is not divided by door tracks: this is a seamless interior, where mechanisms – music, air conditioning, electric blinds and lighting – are hidden.

***Right*** A view of the adjacent dining, living and media rooms; different accent colours are used to highlight the various areas. Detail is added to the spare, edited rooms by the shadow gap at the top of each wall.

CASE STUDY | 1

# indoor outdoor

*In the chic Uccle district of Brussels, the interior of the penthouse-plus-top-floor apartment of a retired Dutch barrister and his wife was designed by Belgian architect Vincent Van Duysen, known for his austere aesthetic and quality. The exterior architect was Belgian Marc Corbiau.*

**Carrara marble and dark oak** form the palette through most of the space. Sliding walls, some in oak, others in glass, carve the penthouse into a variety of configurations, but in essence it is a one-bedroom open-plan dwelling. A marble spiral staircase leads to the lower level, where guest quarters and offices form more of a grouping of rooms.

The dining room extends from the upper-level entry, with a sight line to the trees outside. I think this is the prettiest picture window I have seen since I came across the prototype at the Villa Malaparte on Capri. As a picture frame, it creates a focal point to the space, allowing the peaceful view to take over, so that eating here is almost like dining outdoors – nothing gets in the way of a tranquil dining experience. This home could belong to anyone of any generation. Non-prescriptive, it will stand the test of time.

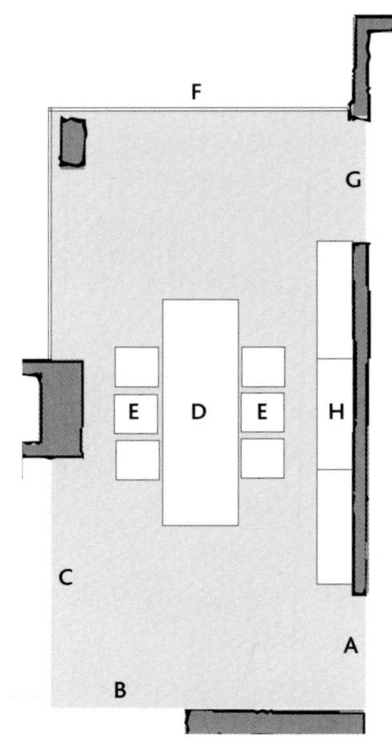


- **A** Entry from hallway
- **B** Open-plan to media room
- **C** Open-plan to living room
- **D** Dining table
- **E** Dining chairs
- **F** Wall-sized picture window
- **G** Entry to kitchen
- **H** Cupboards behind sliding doors

***This page*** Van Duysen wanted to lose this table and chairs and replace the table with a marble slab rising from the ground; the owner forbade this, saying his furniture represented his life. The couple's collection of furniture classics by Eames, Bertoia and Eileen Gray was a new and unusually refined challenge for Van Duysen.

CASE STUDY | 2

## flowing space *In a duplex in a former industrial building in New York's SoHo, designed for clients by David Piscuskas, careful attention was given to the flow of space, and curves were utilised to humanise the otherwise stark area. The result is at once serene, purposeful and playful.*

**The upstairs dining room** acts as a passageway through the space; almost an anti-dining-room rather than a room as such, it gives voice to the modern tendency to eat on the move, and this is what makes it work as a dining room of today. The furniture, although beautiful and solid, does not anchor the space but encourages movement and behaves as sculpture throughout. This is an art-lover's home, in which the home is the art.

The New York firm 1100 Architect was founded in 1983 by Piscuskas and Juergen Riehm. At first their work was seen as the vanguard of a design movement known for its "absence of style" – meaning absence of period and provenance, as opposed to absence of taste! – and an aesthetic of sensuous restraint. Latterly, the lack of signature style has become a style in itself: well-honed, definitive elements, elegant proportion using clean but not minimal lines. Space and sculptural furniture work together.

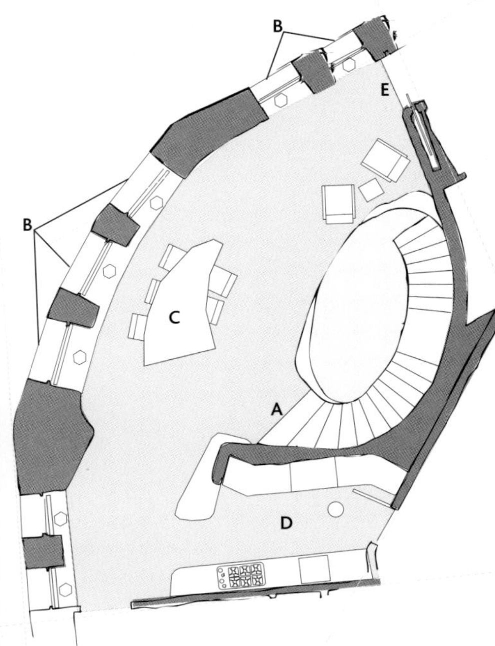


**A** New, curved staircase
**B** Windows
**C** Maple and steel table
**D** Galley kitchen
**E** Entry to rooms beyond

***Far left*** Light, space and the nearby staircase add to the dining room's sense of movement. The windows are original to the building (oak-framed inside) and walls have been painted white.

***Left*** The curved dining table in stained maple hardwood and steel was created specially for this room by Gregory Higgins of Los Olivos, California, Although an afterthought, it claims the space in a unique manner. The chairs are reminiscent of the Greek *klismos* form, which has had many resurgences through history, and was very over-exposed in Georgian times. Floors are poured and scored concrete, tinted greyish.

***This page*** The bronze chandelier is an antique from Sweden; real candles add a romantic quality to the setting, although the dining table is cleverly lit by concealed lamps above, controlled with a dimmer switch "that creates a great effect through the glass in combination with the candles", says Ratia.

**tonal** *Kristiina Ratia has created her American home with the spirit of clarity found in her Finnish homeland, taking inspiration too, if indirectly, from Marimekko, the textile company founded in Helsinki in 1951 by her parents. In her Connecticut house the combination of symmetry and muted colour tones has produced a dining room that is comfortable and not too highly strung, a family room as livable-in as a cashmere sweater.*

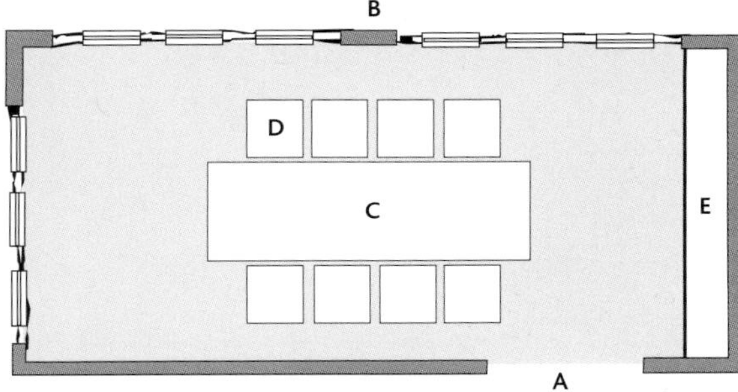


**A** Entry from hallway
**B** Sash windows
**C** Dining table
**D** Dining chairs
**E** Sideboard

***Above*** Well-chosen objects of disparate origin accessorise the sideboard. The round mirror, from Ralph Lauren Home Collection, enforces the symmetry of the room, offset by old English silver and a pair of mercury lamps from *c.*1940 (one seen here). The antique dining table (early twentieth century) contrasts effectively with the sideboard.

***Left*** The sideboard, from Ikea, has been customised with matte black paint. On modern furniture, mechanisms often glide smoothly and drawers fit well. All crockery and glasses are stored away, leaving the room urbanely simple.

**All surfaces in Ratia's dining room** are the same eggshell colour, but the ceiling is in matte finish and the woodwork gloss. The floor is polished oak, stained with her own mix of colour, and the dining chairs are white, covered in a handwoven plain silk from Ratia's collection, with the legs painted black gloss. It is not just the colour and texture palette that make this room comfortable to live in but its symmetry. Although all slightly different thanks to the handwoven silk, the army of chairs is evenly positioned and pert in form, the simplicity exaggerating the room's symmetry.

It is a world away from Marimekko's bold, graphic, colourful fabrics: checked patterns and colossal non-figurative shapes that revolutionised textile printing, described as "garments in a class with industrial design". While influenced by her background, Ratia is a product and interior designer with her own look – and mother of four and former supermodel. Could life be much better?

CASE STUDY | 4

# **transparency** *In the 1950s California began to embrace post-and-beam constructions that allowed in as much light as possible. This house in the Hollywood Hills was created by architect Bob Boulder Thorgusson for a fair in Orange County, and became his own home.*

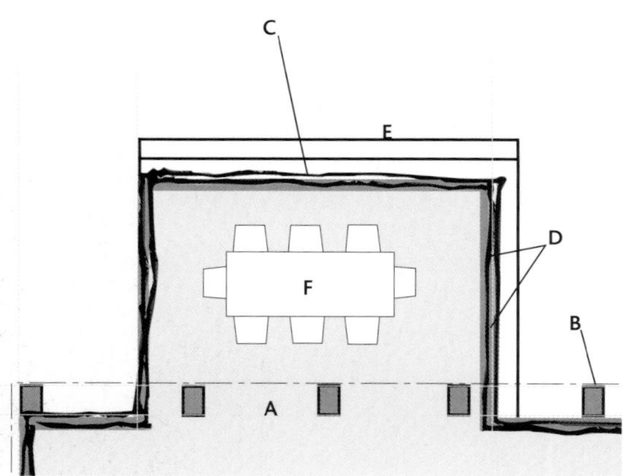

**A wood-and-glass construction** on a hillside, with a pool running underneath parts of the four principal quadrangles and fountains at the rear, the house was one of only a handful by Boulder Thorgusson, whose firm Smith & Williams was better known for industrial and commercial builds. It now belongs to fashion house Juicy Couture's owner, Pam Skaist Levy, and her husband, a film-maker. The couple purchased it in dilapidated state and spent in excess of two years restoring and extending it sensitively, working with Los Angeles-based Argentinian architect Leonardo Chalupowicz.

The entire dining room is a glass box, and the present owner has taken the theme further by using transparent furniture: a custom-made Plexiglass table and chairs. This is a crystal of a room, a pleasant and decorous place to be; it is also practical and comfortable, with all furniture at exactly matched height, and adjacent to the kitchen – an important factor when there are few surfaces to put things on in the dining room.

**A** Entry from hallway between posts
**B** Post-and-beam construction
**C** Glass walls
**D** Stained-glass panels
**E** Outdoor deck
**F** Plexiglass table and chairs

***Above*** The strips of darkened stained glass, in three floor-to-ceiling panels, are an original feature of the house appearing only in the dining and hallway areas. Plain glass vases were carefully selected for their bold scale.

***Right*** The dining room, overhanging the hillside, opens off the hallway; two of the wooden columns that support the house mark the boundary. Plexiglass furniture offers complete transparency, with no hint of green.

# in the kitchen

The great Minimalist of today is John Pawson, but art expert David Gill tells me that the father of the movement was Robert Morris. In 1964 at New York's Green Gallery, Morris exhibited a suite of large-scale polyhedron forms constructed from two-by-fours and grey-painted plywood. The simple geometric sculpture came to be called Minimalist because it seemed to be stripped of extraneous distractions such as figural or metaphorical reference, detail or ornament, and even surface inflection. Morris's mid-1960s sculptures often comprised industrial and building materials such as steel, fibreglass and plywood, and were fabricated commercially to the artist's specifications. The unique gesture, therefore, that defines an individual's skill, the artist's hand, was inimical to Morris, and the work of art became, in theory, a representation of the idea from which it was conceived, as opposed to an "original object". This notion allowed for the creation and hence destruction of the piece when necessary, meaning it could be remade each time it was to be exhibited. Take this notion, also, as the birthplace of the modern prefabricated kitchen: a ready-made concept re-created and tailored for each application.

Morris and his contemporaries, Eva Hesse and Richard Serra, then began in the late 1960s to explore more unusual industrial materials – felt, rubber and wire. Morris particularly went on to explore Anti Form (which speaks for itself), Process Art (which emphasises the process of making art) and Post Minimalism (which often reflected personal and social concerns – it was deemed too "feminine" and "soft" to be Minimalism).

How does all this relate to kitchens? For one thing, the kitchen of today is edited down. Purity is what counts, just as purity of flavour counts in today's cuisine, and the ideal is to highlight rather than smother tastes and functions: a Minimalist approach. So we have no more pots and pans than we need – although we select the best – and furniture is limited to perhaps bar stools at a workstation. In kitchens now, the prime feature is the central workstation: clutter has moved off the walls, various functions are gathered close together, anyone working in the room has plenty of space around them, and if more than one person is using the room it is easier to face each other and be sociable. The kitchen's evolution from the positioning of utilities around the perimeter to the now-ubiquitous central workstation has been helped by the fact that the plumbing remains static but has simply, through fad, moved location to accommodate all facilities in a single unit.

Furthermore, as with Minimalist art, a kitchen is no longer just that. It is a room, an art form, a sculpture, a concept (it can even be a passageway, a non-room). In this chapter we explore a Minimal example (by Vincent Van Duysen), one based upon geometric form (Mark Rios), one that could be said to reflect personal concern (Eric Gizard) and the soft (but not entirely feminine) kitchen of Jasper Conran. The preparation and serving of food have become once again part of the social interaction of our lives, something to be exhibited and appreciated in front of our guests before pulling up a chair. Food and kitchens have become a new art form.

**elemental** *Californian Mark Rios's projects embody a cohesive holistic design philosophy. Being both an architect and a landscape architect, he can provide services indoors and out, leading to detail-oriented and sensitive designs. "The best projects have a crossover range," he says.*

***Above*** Colour and layout are used in a painterly manner reminiscent of Gerrit Rietfeld, who was inspired by art by Piet Mondrian and the Dutch De Stijl group. The cabinets are painted wood; the countertops are Corian.

***Above right*** The floor is custom-made terrazzo, evoking Californian mid-twentieth-century architecture. In contrast to the kitchen, "bar"-area cabinetry is walnut.

***Opposite*** Plain sheet glass increases light and opens up the house. The upper shelving between kitchen window and sliding door is a combination of walnut and painted wood. Dishes on the shelves are by notNeutral.

**According to Rios,** when both interior and exterior professionals are involved in a project, they should agree on the area five feet on either side of the door jambs. Light is important to both disciplines, and he looks at the relationship of colours and texture from indoors to outdoors: "Often you will see cold light on the landscape, which creates a strong disconnect between interior and exterior spaces." As with earlier Los Angeles architects, like Richard Neutra, Rios's work is a continuous discourse between taking the indoors out and bringing the great outdoors in. Neutra claimed that continuity could be maintained by carrying terrazzo flooring from living area to patio, so a house becomes a controlled environment caught behind glass between floor and roof. For Rios too,

A Entry from living area
B Entry from passageway
C Stainless-steel units
D Painted wood units
E Sheet-glass window
F Dining niche
G Bar area

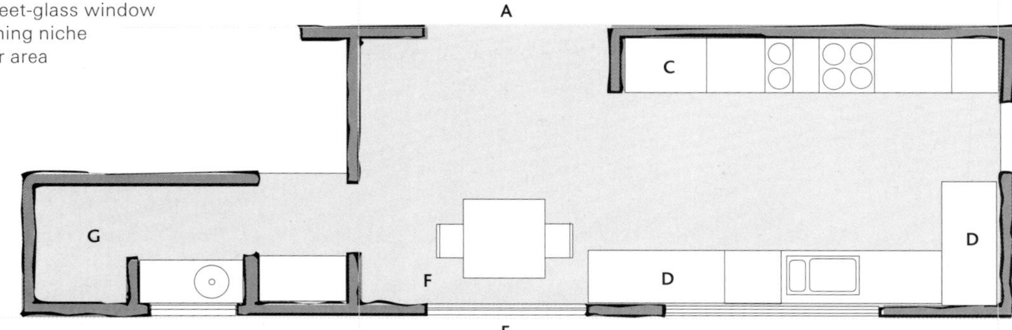


***Right*** Countertops and splashbacks around the range and refrigerator are stainless steel (the fridge is a Sub-Zero), a material which appears on only one side of the kitchen. Each plane is healthily stabilised by dramatic statement: the terrazzo, the use of colour, the dark wood.

***Below*** The dining niche in the kitchen. After World War II, it became more common for kitchen and dining room to be linked, or one within the other.

materials provide great potential for cross-pollination. If a site has stone walls, he might use a honed or cleft equivalent for another surface, such as the floor, inside.

In Rios's own own Bel Air home, interior walls extend to greet the outside. The house is a paintbox of colour, and a homage to the Contemporary style, which, free of the rigours of Modernist theorising but employing much of its basic vocabulary, manifested itself in architecture in the picture window and open plan, lending a striking sense of space and light to the domestic interior.

Continuation of line and form, from inside to out, guides the small buffet kitchen, despite the fact that, in contrast to the magnificent views on the other side of the house, it gives on to the road, with other houses close by. The kitchen continues the house's aesthetic, and is extremely sophisticated in terms of materials too, but it is inconspicuous, a service base for two dining areas rather than a social hub in itself. One dining area is tucked away within the kitchen; the other, only slightly less casual, forms part of the main living space. In addition to the dining niche, the kitchen runs into a "bar" area, so the small space has to be divided effectively into several functions. Creating a sense of division without physical barriers is one of the great challenges of contemporary interior design.

VIKING

# soft modernism

*Exuding a modern grandeur in its combination of classical elegance and soft-edged modernism, Jasper Conran's west London home reflects the stringent nature evident in his designs, whether clothing or products – the "J" line for Debenhams stores, glassware for Waterford, crockery for Wedgwood. His kitchen is an edition of himself.*

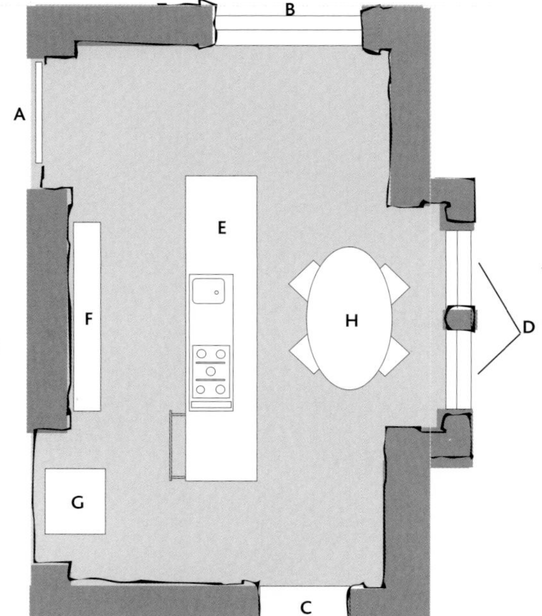


**A** Entry from hallway
**B** Door to built-in traditional cupboard
**C** Entry to salon
**D** Windows
**E** Central workstation
**F** Cantilevered storage unit
**G** Refrigerator
**H** Period table and chairs

**Reconfiguration of the space**, a single floor of a late-Victorian house originally built for the governor of the Bank of England, was essential. The original smaller kitchen has become a bathroom-cum-dressing room; the huge living room was previously a ballroom and called for some overscaled furniture. The new kitchen bravura, once an annexe to the ballroom, had to follow suit. Ann Boyd, who helped design the home, said the main inspiration for texture and detail came from Conran's portrait collection – the details of the lace and fabric in the subjects' clothing.

The kitchen has two entrances, one from the current living room, the other into the entrance hall. It relies on a central island. This is the most popular choice for a workstation in a kitchen of modern manners: it promotes ease of moving around and fluidity. The centrally positioned workstation helps reduce accidents in the home, too.

***Left*** In an effortless medley, the lacquer and stainless-steel kitchen units, by Boffi, are teamed with 1940s chairs. White-painted wooden plantation blinds hang the length of the windows; Venetian blinds would have been too ordinary, curtains too stuffy.

***This page and left, below*** Parallel to the central island, a second, single cantilevered unit runs along the wall; above it a minimal flat steel bar upon which essential utensils hang from hooks. The flooring is wide-plank oak. Constantly battling between modernism and classicism, Conran can hardly be called minimalist: the ornamental stucco wedding-cake effect on walls and ceilings was "inspired by Adam but bought by the yard", as Conran puts it, but retains the character of the place.

***This page*** The line of the central cabinet and the rectangular block above (containing strip lights and air-evacuation unit) are as unembellished as possible. Two prim square sinks are cut from the marble, its sides extending above the countertop as a lip in case of spillage (heaven forbid).

***Right, above*** The oven (large enough for an entire animal) is concealed behind sliding doors, as are cupboards for food and crockery. This is a kitchen that is used heavily – the wife enjoys cooking and her husband's health regime means experimentation and fresh produce reign.

***Right, below*** Kitchen as sculpture. Undeniably Minimalist, this kitchen does not have the sterile quality often associate with pared-down interiors; it is clearly actively lived in.

**bare facts** *Here, in Belgium, in the sublime marble-clad Brussels apartment designed by Van Duysen, we have a small, narrow, marble-clad kitchen with just a central workstation. The unit, like Robert Morris's work from the mid-1960s, delineates the space, and so defines the physical and temporal relationship of the viewer to the sculptural object.*

**A** Entry from hallway
**B** Entry to dining room
**C** Marble walls
**D** Marble workstation and ceiling-mounted extractor
**E** Sliding doors concealing cabinetry and oven
**F** Windows

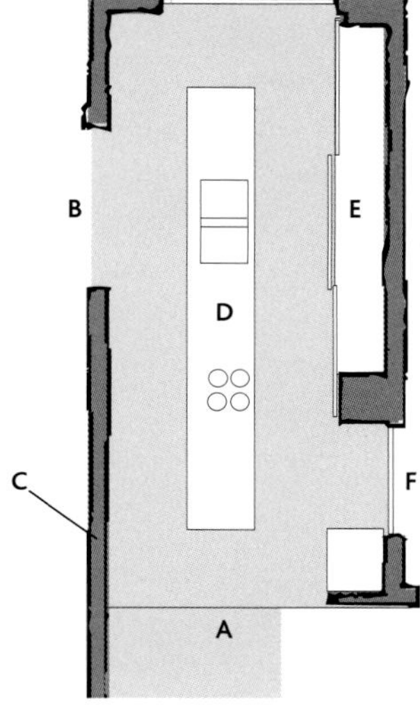

**The central station** is almost a toolbox, the most basic of forms holding all the right implements for the job. In this case, it services a room that is purely functional for preparing food, not for the eating of it – the dining room is adjacent. Is this excessive Minimalism? I think not, because it does work in this serene apartment, which is consecrated to the worship of light (diffused softly by automatically controlled window blinds) and its owners' pure sentiment.

I look at this kitchen and see a vision of something worth hanging on a wall. It is an unenviable task trying to describe in words the hidden expression of say, a multilayered Ben Nicholson piece, or a white-on-white relief by British art duo Langlands and Bell. The art usually speaks for itself. Duysen's marble kitchen for me is the same: words cannot describe its purity. Except, dare I say it, it is classy.

# **personal colour** *Eric Gizard's own home, in contrast to his London clients' (see pages 32–3), has evolved over time, and is indicative of his passion for living with objects from the mid-twentieth century onwards. The colour scheme is dominated by yellow, which works well for most functions.*

**As long as the vision is big,** the budget need not be. Gizard lives on a small, busy street in Paris's tenth arrondissement, a lively location with masses of character. How better to reflect that, and a youthful age (for such an established interior designer), than by creating a spirited, colourful home?

The open-plan apartment is arranged into function groupings. The kitchen has almost ceiling-height storage units, whose backs serve as the entry-hall wall. The opposing kitchen wall is a floor-to-ceiling barrier between bathroom and kitchen, with a large window. Segments of the apartment are defined by differing colour and texture of flooring and walls. The yellow used on the kitchen ceiling, offset by steel grey and blue, is expansive, optimistic and vitalising, unifying the room despite its many functions and facets.

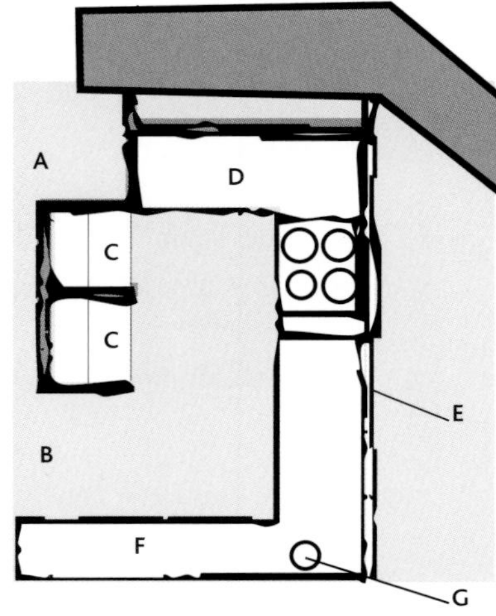


**A** Entry hall
**B** Entry to open-plan kitchen
**C** Refrigerator, oven and storage unit
**D** Ceiling-height storage units
**E** Window to bathroom
**F** Counter between kitchen and dining area
**G** Supporting column

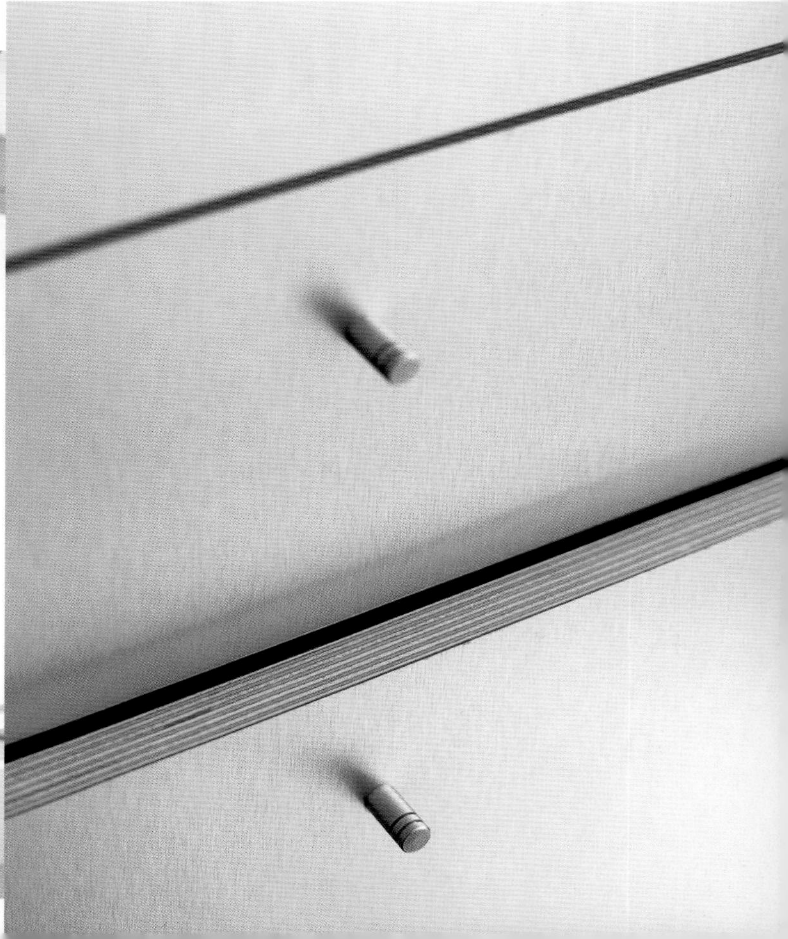

***This page*** The double-globe basketweave lamp has echoes of the 1960s, but is contemporary from Thailand, produced for the company Assiatide. Using colour on the ceiling, with white walls, lowers the ceiling in the mind's eye – not a problem where the modern horizontal box reigns. Supporting columns are necessary and add character.

***Far left*** The kitchen side of the storage system is steel clad. Food is served across the low countertop into the living room, separated from the dressing and bed corner by a floating wall. Contrasting textures are the only decoration.

***Left*** To continue the metallic theme, drawers are clad in metal sheet. Solid metal drawers can be noisy and, unless extremely heavy, appear flimsy. This is a good solution: it fits the theme but is easy on the hand.

# in the connecting space

It was the nineteenth-century Leo Tolstoy in *War and Peace* who, foreshadowing Le Corbusier, first declared, "Our body is a machine for living. It is organised for that, it is its nature. Let life go on unhindered and let it defend itself, it will do more than if you paralyse it by encumbering it with remedies."

We are what we are. In these times of increased self- and other analysis we have acquired yet another buzzword to pinpoint mental state: pathology. The meaning of "pathology" in current times seems to have moved from being the study of changes in tissues and organs, a deviation from the normal healthy state, to being our make-up, our mental or emotional sensitivity or receptiveness, something that cannot be helped. It is as if pathology is the new excuse for eccentricity and peculiarity, even dullness, its semantic proximity to "pathos" alone arousing understanding and pity. Well, if the living, dining, sleeping and bathing sectors of our homes collectively represent our behaviour, then the hallways, stairwells and connecting spaces are the "pathology", built, in general, with material evolved out of necessity. They are what they are. We cannot help but have junctions and traffic routes within our domiciles because we have, first of all, legs and, secondly, options.

Hallways and connecting spaces are fundamental to how a home works, and staircases – without which there would be no upper floors – play a major part, changing in form as materials evolve. Clay and straw, the first materials used for staircases, quickly gave way to stone and timber. From the nineteenth century, steel and concrete made it possible to bridge enormous physical and metaphorical gaps, and glass, reinforced concrete and modern advances in construction techniques play an increasing role in opening audacious architectural possibilities. With diverse use of building materials, staircases lost their rigidity: spatial spiral silhouettes and extreme curves became fashionable. Today materials are less relevant; we focus on the inherent character of the staircase, its form and innate function of going up and down. Staircases, like connecting spaces, have simplified, at least in appearance, while banisters and the steps themselves give a modern staircase individuality.

Options for connecting spaces are innumerable: a home may have a hallway that functions as a hub for other rooms, may comprise a series of consecutive rooms, with a corridor along the side serving as a string from which they hang, or may be opened up so that rooms are interconnected and there is no hallway at all. If a hallway exists, it may be merely a transit area, or an activity centre and a room in its own right. Whatever the case, a hallway benefits from appropriate lighting (natural or unnatural), and its materials are fundamental to its being. Your choices must be dictated by your needs – whether you live alone, share with others, have to accommodate children (therefore noise) and consider safety – and require a combination of analysis, understanding who you are, and feeling. Instinct can solve many of the problems, as recognised by American composer Michael Torke, quoted in *The Observer*: "Why waste money on psychotherapy when you can listen to Bach's *B Minor Mass*?"

CASE STUDY | 1

**openness** *British-based American architect Michael Wolfson, who studied in London at the Architectural Association in Bloomsbury, describes his work as "a deconstructed Modernism, although it is really an advancement of the theories and ideals Modernism sprang from".*

***Above*** The living areas are united visually with wide-plank limed-oak floors from Poland and physically by a grand but Minimalist staircase, the architectural focus of the house, which winds around a wall pierced with rectangular holes that reduce its volume. The wall conceals the steel structure vital to support the stairs.

***Above right*** The client kept asking for "more light" and insisted on more openings.

***Opposite*** The second floor opens on to the dining room, a half-level below, and the studio, a half-level above.

**Form, line and texture** are Wolfson's main interests; these are themes that become particularly evident in the connecting spaces between rooms, and which Wolfson has applied effectively to the London home of Prince Nicholas Guedroitz and his wife Solina, a photographer. Together with their three children, they are based in London because they enjoy the city and because the prince's business is here: he is an expert in Russian antiques and artefacts, which appear in his Pimlico Road gallery. The couple needed a sizable house which would sensibly accommodate family needs yet form a contemporary backdrop to many of the older pieces they collect. Their classic Kensington townhouse has been transformed by Wolfson into a masterpiece of shifted space: the

***Opposite*** A view from the living room to the dining room a half-level below (the facing wall is mirrored), with studio above. The sight line maximises light. These dining-room chairs are eighteenth-century French, the steel-and-glass table by Sir Norman Foster for the Italian firm Techno.

***Left*** A view from the studio. Opening up the hallway created a gallery-like area whose occupants can have their own space without being isolated from others.

main body of the house has been gutted, so that it is now practically open-plan, its framework altered beyond recognition. The entire principal space has become a collection of free-flowing rooms, drawn as if in a continuous line.

Entry into the home opens on to a magnificent staircase which ushers the visitor directly up into the dining room – as if on a mezzanine, with a terrace beyond. A few more steps up and you are projected quickly and quietly into the living room, which leads to another mezzanine that acts as a studio. The area is wholly interconnected, yet each space finds its privacy.

This middle, primary section of the house billows between the other two thirds, the upper and lower levels. A hidden staircase leads to the upper floors, which hold the bedrooms; in the basement are service rooms for staff, while the ground floor is more den than formal, and includes the original library, preserved for its wonderful proportions. The whole is linked by a very open space that encourages free movement of occupants; as the ancient Greek philosopher Heraclitus said, "All is flux, nothing stays still."

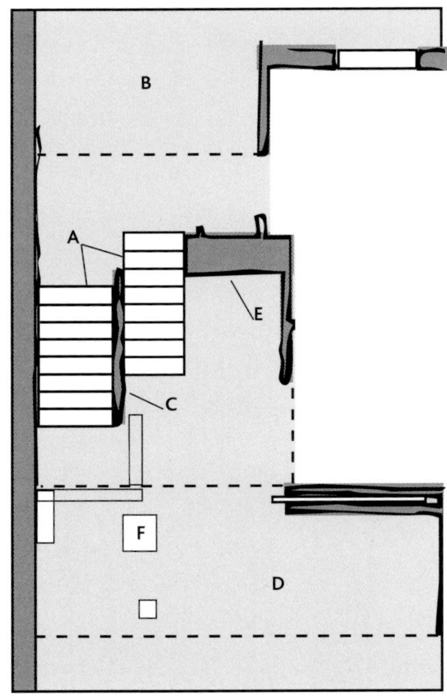


**A** Staircase
**B** Dining room
**C** Short wall with cut-outs
**D** Living room
**E** Mirrored wall
**F** Support

CASE STUDY | 2

## central access

*Where many open-plan homes have no hallway, more a collective grouping of space with axes in all directions, Pam Skaist Levy's house in the Hollywood Hills (restored by Leonardo Chalupowicz) is open-plan yet centres around its entrance hall, which is very much part of the living space.*

**The seamlessness of this house** is expressed through the polished wooden and slate floors washing through the entrance hall (which acts as a room in itself), the dining room (see pages 42–3) and the living room. These three spaces are interconnected, with no doors. All walls in the house are essentially glass panels with timber frames, emphasising the natural materials (despite the industrial mood, with structure on show). The sounds from the waterfalls and fountains add Japanese-type peacefulness, and Skaist Levy designed most interior elements in the house on a Japanese/American model; "James Bond meets Kyoto," is how she describes it.

This entrance hall is demure in sentiment – one of the smallest, least offensive entrances I have seen in the Los Angeles area. Furniture and decorative elements have been customised to suit the space: the low table fits around a pillar, feeding both hallway and sitting room and anchoring the two spaces together; the candle holder can serve as a focal point in either hallway or dining area.

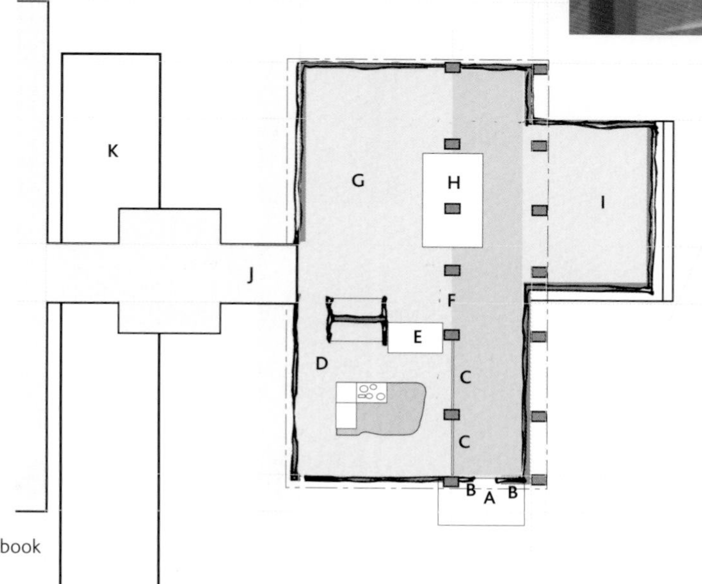


- **A** Front door
- **B** Stained-glass panels
- **C** Sliding shoji screens to kitchen
- **D** Kitchen
- **E** Breakfast bar
- **F** Open access between posts to living room
- **G** Living room
- **H** Table designed around support post
- **I** Dining room, also open to hallway
- **J** Passage to interior bridge
- **K** Swimming pool

***Above*** Every room has at least one beautiful hour – this has more. Its east-west axis means that in the morning it is ignited by the sun, with strong shadows; in the afternoon the light is soft; at dawn it is cold; and at night it appears gilded.

***Right*** The opposite viewpoint, looking from the entrance. The living room is to the left, the dining room past the pillars to the right. Beyond the glass wall is one of the terraces, its greenery echoed in green glassware.

OFFERINGS

CASE STUDY | 3

# linking rooms

*In fashion-photography agency owner and PR supremo Katy Barker's Paris pied-à-terre, rooms trail one after another in the traditional French way, with a connecting edge, a narrow passage at times, sometimes a mere suggestion of a hallway using floor lighting.*

***This page*** A view from the living room indicates how the rooms are partitioned, one following another, fed by a simple narrow corridor to one side. Note floor and ceiling lights. The kitchen is followed by the dining room, then closet space and finally a guest bedroom.

***Opposite*** The opposite view, the photographer turning 180 degrees to face the bathroom, a section of the living room and the stairs to the main bedroom. Clever square recessed floor lights help guide the eye upwards, both useful for seeing (almost a flight path) and a suggestion of welcome. The white chair, one of a pair, is by Arne Jacobsen.

**This Paris apartment** exemplifies one of the great differences between the cultures and living habits of California and those of France: in contrast to the Hollywood Hills house (see pages 62–3), whose hallway is the hub for an open-plan lifestyle, the French traditionally prefer to have separate rooms for different activities. Katy Barker's home is not exactly a traditional French *enfilade* of rooms, which would take the form of one room following another through doors at each juncture, without a corridor running parallel, but the effect is somewhat the same. However, much of this is a result of cultural customs when buildings were built and how we adapt spaces to suit modern needs.

Barker, who is based primarily in London, turned to interior architect Laurent Buttazzoni to reapportion her mainly ground-floor Left Bank pad (there is a bedroom on an upper level at one end of the apartment). The main entry door leads directly into the living room, without any entrance hall, and the passageway towards other rooms stretches along the opposite wall.

This configuration reminds me of the teetering moment between airport lounge and plane: the lounge stretching widthwise, with the corridor to the satellites beyond. At airports this seems to work well since, post security, one no longer feels the need for any more barriers. In Barker's sixth-arrondissement apartment, the feeling is the same; her home is also secured by the luxury of a courtyard, inside the main entrance of the building, crossed prior to being plumped directly into her living room. If this configuration appeared in, say, New York, where there are few interior courtyards, I would not think it practical or sensible at all, too vulnerable to the outside world. Only in the more ancient European cities, where central courtyards exist, is this set-up practicable, the courtyard to the entire building acting as a hallway.

Inside Barker's home, the space is fluid: four white boxes, doorless, with the link between rooms a flight path of lights along the furthest wall. Even this suggestion of a passageway has only as much girth as fire restrictions dictate. Yet it forms a clearly defined linking thread between the separate rooms.

***Below*** With no doors between corridor and kitchen, it is important to keep utility areas neat; this is the view leaving the dining room, en route to the living room. All amenities are stored in a single white laminate and stainless-steel kitchen unit running the length of the interior wall.

***Right*** The apartment has two entry doors: a glass one here (left) and a second in the kitchen, both opening on to the courtyard. The corridor runs along the wall furthest from the entry. The light oak shelves are placed to emphasise the graphic rectilinearity of the space. Sofas are by B&B Italia.

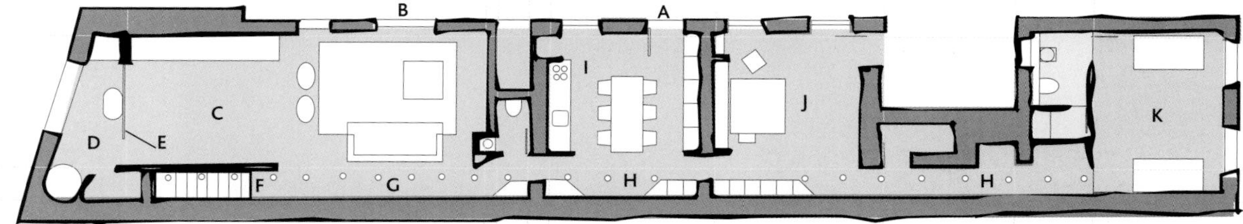


A Entry from courtyard into kitchen
B Entry into living room
C Living room
D Master bathroom
E Glass wall
F Stairs to upper-level bedroom
G Corridor
H Recessed floor lights
I Kitchen
J Dining room
K Guest bedroom and bathroom

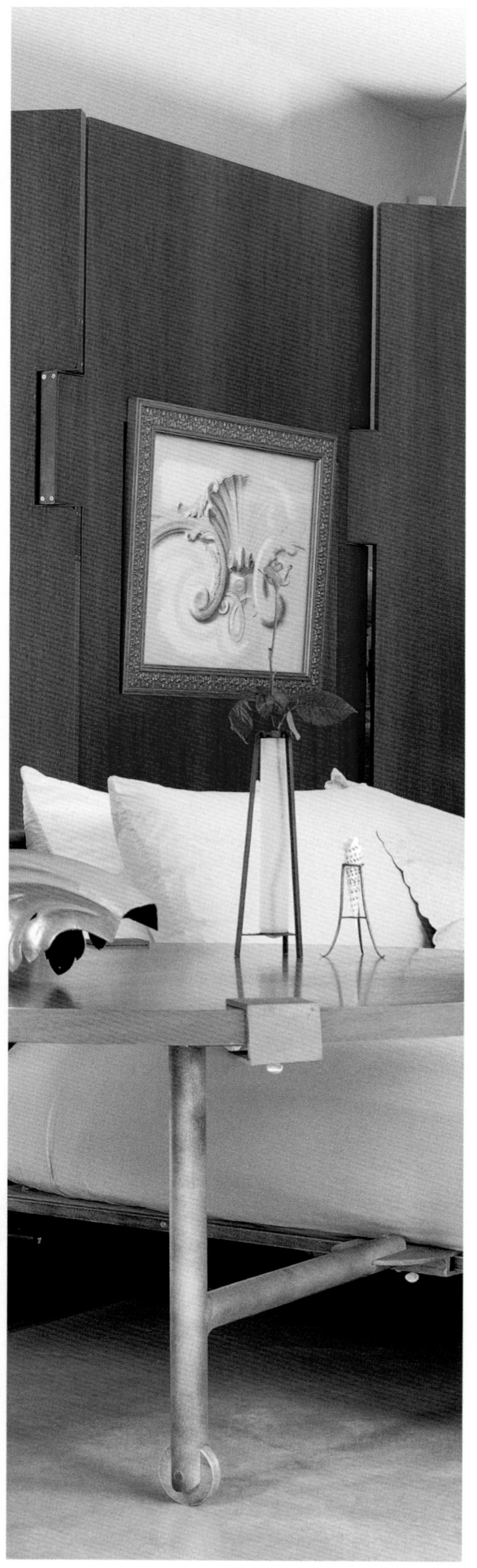

# in the bedroom

G. K. Chesterton, the English essayist, novelist and poet, said in his *Tremendous Trifles* (1909), "Lying in bed would be an altogether perfect and supreme experience if only one had a coloured pencil long enough to draw on the ceiling." This, obliquely, reminds me of a lesson given by my headmaster when I was of a very tender age, which I paraphrase wildly: the definition of hell is a low banqueting table, laden with sweetmeats and mead, a candlelit feast; alas, the characters who find themselves in hell are sitting on high chairs, out of reach of the table, with only long eating implements with which to feed themselves – a scene of starvation, torture and temptation. Cut to heaven, and what is in front of us? Curiously, the same high chairs and low banqueting table laden with the same food, but with one significant difference: those who have found themselves in heaven are gloriously happy and satisfied, for they are using the long implements to feed each other across the table (probably making friends too). The scene is the same, the outlook so different.

And there we have the bedroom. We need a floor, a bed of sorts and walls (these could be optional), and that is about it, but oh how varied can that simple combination become. It is people's attitudes towards sleeping and the bedroom that make an inordinate difference to how they create their shell for sleeping and the satisfaction derived. For some the bedroom is a place of refuge, for others contemplation, for others still, sociability, but it should always be a place where generosity reigns.

That may mean generosity in various terms – size, views or a private bathroom, for instance. Most importantly, the bed should, if possible, have space around three sides, so that getting in and out is trouble-free. A bedroom interior is about action (going to bed) followed by lack of action (sleep), and hopefully, somewhere in between, romance or at least a good read. I imagine Chesterton's bed was comfortable, for drawing on the ceiling is inspired by that moment when nothing else matters, a moment of disengagement from daily life, that only a well-planned bedroom and a well-sprung (in those days, stuffed) mattress bring.

Bedrooms are more private than any other room – more so than bathrooms, since guests see a bathroom once in a while, but not a bedroom. Bedroom details can be more personal. In the bedroom, paintings and mirrors are hung at the inhabitant's head height, rather than at average head height. It is where, if you own many clothes, you can be generous in accommodating them, since your space in your bedroom is your own or, hopefully, shared with someone you care enough about to compromise, just a little.

My husband, a designer, cannot keep furniture of his own design for more than a week. I compromise by accepting the coming and goings of various objects in our home, particularly in the bedroom. His compromise is that he refills only the space he has emptied and no more. Now, I adore his furniture but this is where we meet, in the bedroom particularly. Neither of us draws on the ceiling – yet – but we are comfortable in the knowledge that happiness begins where generosity reigns.

CASE STUDY | 1

# private view *Interior designer John Stedila's weekend home in Amagansett, Long Island, is a country enclave where he comes alone as respite from the mayhem of life in Manhattan. With just one inhabitant, there is no need for segmentation, and only screens subdivide the space.*

**Stedila recognised the "good bones"** of the building – a concrete, peak-roofed shell, formerly a private fire station – but wanted to avoid designing in Amagansett style, which generally means shingle. The upper floor, previously for storage, was dismantled and living-room ceilings were raised. Glass doors now open where the fire doors were.

The only bedroom faces the large, unoverlooked plot of land beside the house; the adjoining shower room also has doors to the garden, which are almost always open for a near-alfresco experience. The great outdoors is the focal point in this home, which is televisionless. Between the living room, bedroom and bathroom there are no doors, just a seamless procession of cosy rooms. When rooms are close together, and visible from each other, it is important to keep elements smart. This bedroom is particularly successful in that the uninterrupted sight line from living room through to the lawn is unencumbered by objects often evident in a personal room, yet it is comfortable.

A Doorless entry from living room
B Mahogany screen concealing storage
C Bed and connecting table
D Doors to garden
E Passage to shower room
F Cantilevered staircase
G Doors from shower to garden

***Right*** The bed, framed by a mahogany screen, is connected to a table that pivots around for eating and reading. It also acts as an occasional table, the brushed-steel leg refined by the wooden tabletop. The three-element grouping gives the bed area a self-contained feeling.

***Far right*** Opposite the window wall, a squared-off bleached-wood stairway leads to a small dressing room. The strict forms of the staircase and linear cabinet are almost sculptural, highly attractive and modern.

***Opposite*** A 1940s French tan leather club chair is the only chair in the room. Its rustic nature offsets the smooth, polished concrete floor. The 1940s-style window and door treatment in steel and glass echoes that in the living room.

# simplicity

*Self-confirmed "Baroque Modernist" architect Sally Mackereth lives with her husband Julian Vogal in a mews house in London's Hampstead. She designed the home herself, finding that it embodied very different challenges from her usual commercial work for clients.*

**Mackereth is co-founder** with James Wells in 1995 of the architectural firm Wells Mackereth, which operates in the commercial sector, in restaurant and store design, where space and light are easier to manipulate. In her own home, Mackereth had to be practical, but proceeded to move walls to create as much space and light as possible. Floors were shifted a few inches and relaid in English oak.

The square upstairs bedroom had to remain as simple as possible, to avoid becoming overwhelming, yet the couple desired a bedroom space that was visually accessible: not entirely minimal, and using materials befitting a mews house rather than an industrial space. The room works because of its warm, well-thought-out simplicity. It is as neat as a ship's galley, the floor left empty and uninhibited by extra furniture or doors (where possible, sliding doors have been used, to maximise space), the unbroken visual horizon anchoring the room.

***Opposite and left*** Although this is not a vast room, the bed is positioned centrally for easy access to the small balcony, through French doors. The low bed is without frills, but warmed up with a coyote-fur throw from Etro. A shelf in English oak with drawers for essentials sits snugly into the corner, suggesting a bed niche. Rare twentieth-century prints rest upon the shelf, another of a unicorn on the floor. The pair of antique lamps were a (welcome) wedding gift and give a trace of identity.

***Left, above*** The floor-to-ceiling white-painted door mimics the sliding door to the bath and shower room on the right. Sliding doors are essential for small spaces; they should glide unnoticed. Note the recessed handles.

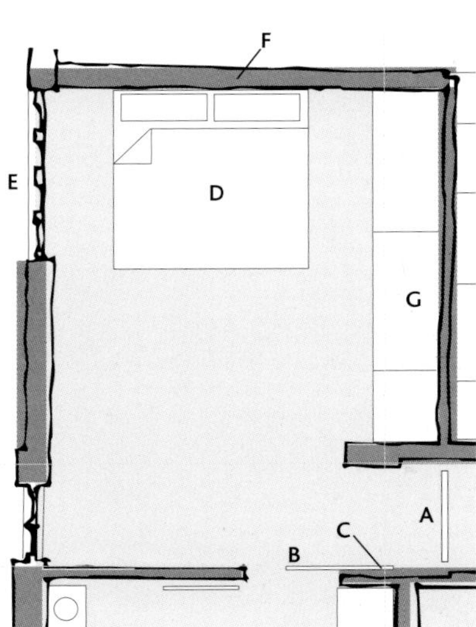


**A** Entry from kitchen
**B** Sliding door to dressing room and shower
**C** Tall, narrow window exposed by sliding door
**D** Bed
**E** Inward-opening doors to balcony (with roller blinds)
**F** Cantilevered shelf above bed
**G** Storage closets

CASE STUDY | 3

# exposed

*Good architecture stems from finding a solution to a problem, preferably an attractive solution. When faced with a Paris apartment in the old Marais quarter, where rooms are narrow, one leading to the next, it seems best to accommodate as much in the space as possible.*

**The lack of space** dedicated to ablution facilities in Paris apartments often bewilders Americans and British, but these dwellings can be old, and many are already chopped up from larger units. The little oblique corner that becomes a toilet facility is all too common in France's capital. So what better solution than to create a room within a room, here a shower in a bedroom? (I hasten to add that the pastime of voyeurism might not be to everyone's taste, but here we have a solution to that problem too.)

The two young architects, Olivier Marty and Karl Fournier, of Paris interior architecture and design company Kold, opened up spaces, removing cornices not original to the building, then introduced floor-to-ceiling doors between rooms and a neutral, almost natural colour palette. Their theatrical display of curtaining, sheer sweeps of white polyester crepe from wall to wall, gives a delightful light play at the window and along inside walls conceals those practical details of living such as clothing storage. The result of the bedroom design is more hotel room than home, which seems to be the aspiration of many young people today with disposable income who are in a position to commission an architect.

***Right*** Blankets, coverlets and quilts are difficult to keep tidy. One solution is to give a vertical seam to the bed end, here an attractive lace-up system. This coverlet was made by Polybe and Malet in ecru wool by fabric company Zimmer and Rohde.

***Centre*** Three of the shower walls are glass, the fourth a mosaic of sugar-coloured *pâte de verre*, as is the shower floor. Cleverly hidden is the vanity unit behind: washbasin, shelves and drawers. The flooring beyond is slats of teak, which is practical and adds texture. Teak is a hardwood that behaves well in humidity and is good for bathrooms, unless cedar is preferred for its subtle odour. The armchair is by Modénature.

***Above*** The bedhead, a panel of light oak, also supports neat cantilevered shelves and drawers. Lighting in the bedroom is controlled by touch panels; additional task lighting, for reading, is provided by the bedside lamps.

- **A** Entry from living room
- **B** Pivoting oak door
- **C** Oak bedhead with cantilevered drawers
- **D** Bed
- **E** Clothing storage behind drapes
- **F** Shower unit
- **G** Washbasin and vanity unit
- **H** Teak-floored washroom area
- **I** French doors to balcony

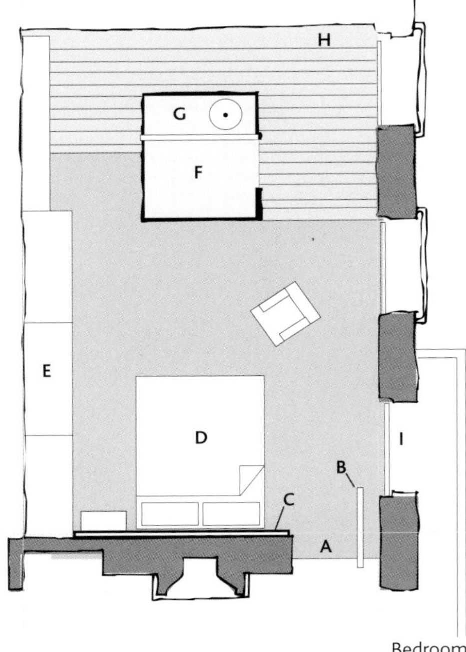

# calm neutrality

*London fashion designer Jasper Conran wanted a one-bedroomed apartment with room for entertaining. His serene home is the result of collaboration with interior designer Ann Boyd, who trained at London's prestigious St Martin's School of Art and also worked in fashion.*

**Boyd's signature style** is based on men's suiting fabrics, such as grey flannel, with crisp white and ivory cottons and linens. Although in London, this apartment has been made more airy, lighter, by using pale colours and fabrics more often associated with life in a warmer climate. Only three shades were used to paint the entire flat, from the Slate 111 range of Architectural Colours from Chelsea's Paint Library; all surfaces in the bedroom are white or subtle grey.

This simplicity of design and Conran's needs from his bedroom have produced a calm space. Original nineteenth-century features remain, and in a grand room with a high ceiling, overscale furniture can be used, evoking extreme comfort; here it brings out the room's natural formality, counterbalancing the informality of the colour palette and textures. The room works not just as a sleeping cell but as somewhere to read, relax and spend time collecting thoughts – and occasionally receive friends informally.

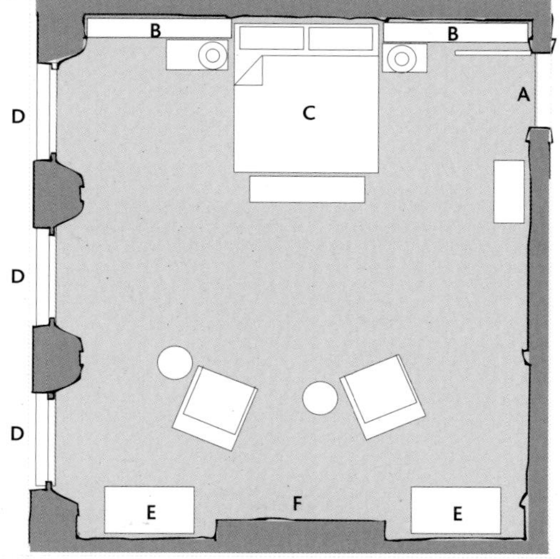


**A** Entry from corridor
**B** Built-in bookcases
**C** Bed, with ottoman at its foot
**D** Full-height windows, with plantation shutters
**E** Walnut cabinets
**F** Fireplace and chimney breast

***Above*** Cabinetry, including two vast walnut closets on cabriole legs, was specially commissioned. The Moroccan inlay table suggests life abroad, as do shutters, and personalises the space. The custom-dyed "Baby Weimaraner" carpet is from Wool Classics.

***Right*** The bed, its pristine headboard upholstered for comfort. is slightly recessed by addition of bookcases as tall as the panel behind. Beds are best central to a room so they can be walked around.

THE ART OF PHOTOGRAPHY
MAN THE ARTIST
ANTONIA FRASER
VIONNET
AFRICA
OSCAR WILDE
KITTY KELLEY
AFRICAN CEREMONIES
AFTER THE WAR WAS OVER
TSUJIGAHANA
SARGENT
VERSAILLES

# in the bathroom

I came across a poem, when sitting in the bath, by seventeenth-century Richard Crawshaw, which was not the most inspiring except for two lines: "Two walking baths; two weeping motions; Portable and compendious oceans." The link between baths and portability set me thinking.

Those who design bathrooms tend not to design fixtures or plumbing, which has meant the evolution of the bathroom is not as advanced as other rooms. In living rooms and bedrooms the designer usually at least decides on the location of electrical sockets, which now appear more readily on the floor than on walls, so wires do not impede flow. Had bathroom designers historically designed plumbing as well, we might by now have bathrooms where the "furniture" is movable. As a living room benefits from repositioning sofas seasonally, a bathroom too could gain from occasional alteration: the bath near a window in summer and close by a radiator in winter. How about a bath in the bedroom? Alas, this flexibility is not yet attainable. A bathroom is a room of inertia, in more ways than the obvious.

In contrast to the kitchen, in the bathroom a central "station" is not appropriate, since different ablutions do not lead from one to another, nor is it an appealing option. Also, a bathroom needs mirrors, usually best placed on walls – although they can be attractive on columns. I do think, however, that there is more scope for radical change than we are currently attempting. Aside from plumbing, it appears low tech is the future for the washing facility, and despite the cry "low concept, high impact" – simple concept with great effect – from young designers, my belief is that the bathroom, no matter how simple it turns out, begins with a very high concept indeed, which translates into simplicity and eventually high impact.

A bathroom is anchored by gravity: water flows downwards and we have to accommodate it in floor-level (bath) and waist-level (basin) vessels. Nothing could be simpler, in theory, but it so often goes wrong. The following bathrooms are exemplary of well-thought-out space: baths large enough to bathe in yet not difficult to negotiate; basins, or fashionable troughs, that are also water features, their gentle trickling part of a calm environment. Mirrors are within vision reach (not blocked by a huge basin surround) and, importantly, lighting and heating have been resolved. A good bathroom can be expensive, but should be a room you wish to revisit, again and again. It is a sanctuary, and nothing, but nothing, must disturb its purity of spirit or its form.

Since bathrooms require a certain amount of fixed floor-level furniture, it is imperative not to add more. Closets that shut away the clutter of make-up and accessories should be cantilevered; shelves should extend elegantly from wall to wall or unit to unit.

The bathroom is usually the most pared-down room in a contemporary home, the materials therefore of paramount importance. Durability is key; materials with a short lifespan are useless. Marble, slate, stone, ceramic or glass tile, stainless steel and porcelain all are welcome. Woods work very well too, visually; some (cedar) smell delicious in heat whether damp or dry, and teak and other tropical hardwoods are excellent for humid environments.

**elevated space** *Not far from Lille in France, the town of Roubaix is home to interior architect Jean-Marc Vynckier, whose sizable loft (over 500 square metres/5,000 square feet) is a former ironing room in a dyeing factory. His objective was to create atmosphere from a potentially bland environment.*

***Above*** In the main bathing area, a floating wall acts as backdrop to the bathtub, which is set in a long platform surround that looks like a piece of furniture. The architect is not only creating a platform for informal chat while bathing but echoing the line of the wall, which is the same length, giving visual harmony and balance.

***Above right*** Behind the floating marble vanity unit is the section of the bathroom which holds the bathtub. The lamps are by Philippe Starck for Artemide.

**The architect's starting point** is consideration of the space and its potential for light, but this generosity to space and light is not ostentatious. Texture and colours on wall and floor surfaces include the Moroccan *tadelak* (a swirling stucco finish to walls) and use of a re-edition of Le Corbusier's paint palette. Vynckier likes to use modern materials: concrete, glass, aluminium.

This L-shaped loft is essentially open-plan, but sections remain fairly private due to the sheer volume of the space and a few subdividing walls, although there are no interior doors. In the sleeping and bathing section, in the shorter leg of the L configuration, is a blue-lit dressing room (designed rather like a fashion store), behind which sits the

***This page*** Cut from a slab of white marble, the trough is a divider between bathroom and bedroom. Its taps are by Andrée Putman. The intimate nature of the bathing regime is suggested by the deep-bordeaux-coloured curtains at the window.

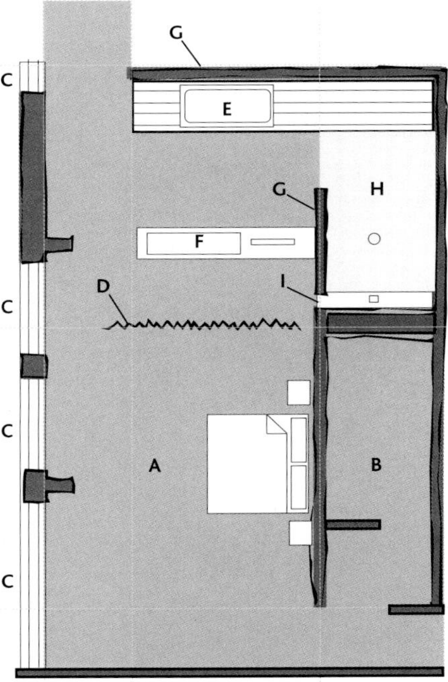


**A** Bedroom
**B** Neon-lit dressing room
**C** Windows to inner courtyard
**D** Curtains separating bedroom and bathroom
**E** Bath and lengthy wooden surround, on floating wall
**F** Marble washing trough and vanity unit, on floating wall
**G** Floating walls
**H** Shower room
**I** Gap in wall

***Left*** The shower walls are finished in mottled greyish *tadelak*, executed by the Belgian firm Adilon Courtrai; the blue light stems from the neon-lit dressing room beyond. Note the two generous shower domes. Detailing around the filter on the floor, the recess, is both elegant and functional.

***Above*** Behind the wall to the right is the dressing room, which backs on to the shower. The curtains pull back to reveal the marble vanity unit at eye level and trough at waist height, beyond which is the bath.

master bedroom; this in turn leads to the spacious bathroom and shower area, open-plan to the bedroom save for generous wall-length white parachute curtaining that can be swept aside. Two doorways (without doors) lead from the passage beyond the bathroom to more sleeping quarters. Dividing walls fall short of the ceiling, purposely to appear as if floating, which gives the architecture an even more pronounced horizontal direction.

One element of bathrooms which has evolved in recent years is the shower: it must be fierce but comforting, the shower domes (as heads are now dubbed) generous, the space generous. This shower area has two entrances: it is possible to walk in by one entrance, through two showers, and exit on the other side. The extra entrance at the end of the shower walls is also an attractive architectural device to open up the shower room, to prevent the configuration appearing too boxy.

Key to this bathroom is its size: it is spacious and open without being bland. So often does a bathroom become smaller than desired; other rooms increase in size because their space is considered more useful. Here, however, the walk-in shower room is large enough for a group of six, or a luxury if one or two. Bathing is elevated to a focal point of life, an indulgent, almost Roman or spalike social experience.

# modern marble

*Paris-based designer Frédéric Méchiche is known for creativity and a desire to mix things primitive with the contemporary. In designing Joël Robuchon's Paris home, Méchiche has created a fluid contemporary space.*

**A 1950s building that has been transformed** into a duplex, opening everywhere on to terraces, the apartment is ostensibly open-plan, created for a single man who likes to stay home, to cook and entertain. Its relatively small bathroom functions well for a single occupant who nevertheless likes beautiful things. The most delicious aspect of this bathroom is the vision behind it: when seated in the bath, all mirrors are positioned so the Eiffel Tower is reflected in each and every one. Méchiche, a self-confessed perfectionist who spent his childhood in Algeria and Switzerland, describes it as "modern luxury". The bathroom design makes the most of Carrara marble, which has a slightly fawn tone to it, softer on the eye than white marble, and thus works well in a warm contemporary home. Although marble is thought to be cold, it behaves well in bathrooms: it takes time to warm up, but it then retains its heat and is slow to cool down.

***Far left*** The tiles are handcut Carrara marble, the frieze at the top of the room and the floor border black marble. The basin and bath are also Carrara marble, the bath cut from a single slab. Recessed cupboards each side of the basin sit flush with the wall, disappearing into it.

***Left*** The chrome-surround mirrors were custom designed by Méchiche, who also designed the lights to emit kind but useful light. The milk glass filters light evenly, so faces are neither top- nor under-lit.

***Above*** The cross-shaped taps are called "Tara", by Dornbracht. A popular choice, in my experience they are very easy to handle with wet hands (and no matter what size of hands). The arch of the spout is elegant, not too blunt.

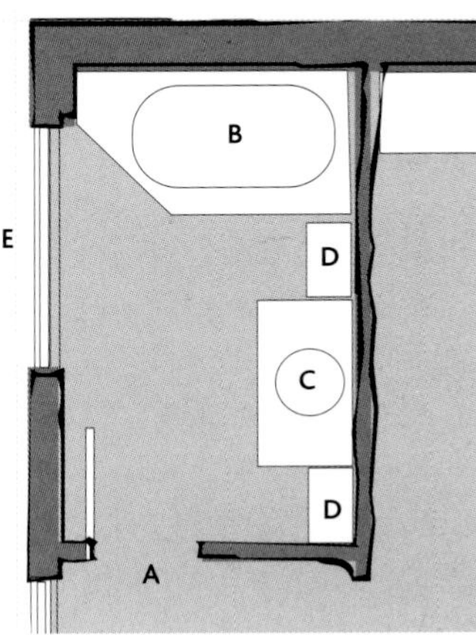


**A** Entry from hallway
**B** Marble bath
**C** Marble basin
**D** Tile-clad concealed storage, with mirrored fronts
**E** Window with plain glass

CASE STUDY | 3

# urban logic

*The home created by Belgian architect François Marcq for a businessman whose life stands for order, on the appropriately named Quai de l'Industrie in the very centre of Brussels, is exemplary of good interior architecture today. It is functional and attractive, and not too overblown.*

***Right*** In the refurbished open-plan loft, the bath has a central station overlooking the main space from the mezzanine gallery. The floor is stained oak, and the bath is clad in the same oak.

***Far right*** The bathroom is above the kitchen, supported by the exposed structural "I" beams. The steel bridges lead to the bedroom, on a mezzanine above the living domain. Symmetry is the theme, with two cubicles; one holds a shower clad in 10-x-10-centimetre (4-x-4-inch) grey tiles.

**With a few years' hindsight,** it is possible to identify the late 1980s as a period of exultant experimentation in contemporary architecture. From the final breath of "post-Modern" pastiche to the tortured volumes of deconstruction, architecture went off in every conceivable direction. When real-estate markets collapsed from California to Japan, a natural swing of the pendulum from euphoria to doubt and increasing sense of social dysfunction, in Europe in particular, played a role in changing 1990s taste.

Suddenly safer and more austere architecture gained popularity. In Holland the geometric concrete of Wiel Arets and Ben Van Berkel became better appreciated. Then, in the mid- to late 1990s, deconstructed Belgian design began to be recognised as a

***This page*** Accessorising is serious business: the basins are by Duravit, the taps designed by Philippe Starck (his signature lozenge shape has become the pull handle). The combination of stainless steel and porcelain is less harsh with addition of oak.

***Opposite*** The large mirror behind the basins was positioned to reflect light. Walls and ceiling are painted stark "builder's" white and the built-in lighting is by specialists Modular. Lighting any room is best left to experts who understand colour theory and physics.

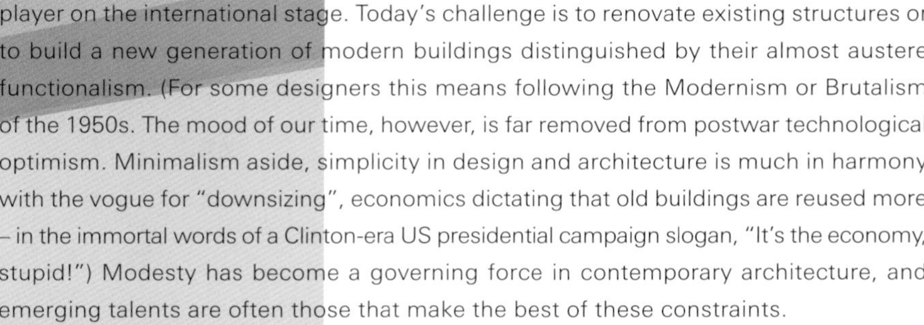

player on the international stage. Today's challenge is to renovate existing structures or to build a new generation of modern buildings distinguished by their almost austere functionalism. (For some designers this means following the Modernism or Brutalism of the 1950s. The mood of our time, however, is far removed from postwar technological optimism. Minimalism aside, simplicity in design and architecture is much in harmony with the vogue for "downsizing", economics dictating that old buildings are reused more – in the immortal words of a Clinton-era US presidential campaign slogan, "It's the economy, stupid!") Modesty has become a governing force in contemporary architecture, and emerging talents are often those that make the best of these constraints.

Belgian architect François Marcq is one such architect who works in a modest and contemporary manner. The home he created (in a building dating from the cusp of the 1950s and 1960s) for his client, a busy businessman who needs order in his home, is an urban creation but acts as respite from urban reality. Although lofty and spacious, the design remains demure and accessible, certainly logical: the materials reflect both nature, in the wood, and the urban landscape, in industrial steel. Nowhere is this more evident than in the bathroom. Even with a decent budget, it is now apropos to keep design fundamental to living.

**A** Staircase from main space up to bedroom
**B** Cross-hatch treadplate steel bridges from bedroom to bathroom
**C** Steel safety handrails
**D** Bath with oak surround
**E** Double vanity unit
**F** Large mirror
**G** Shower room in grey tile
**H** Clothing closets

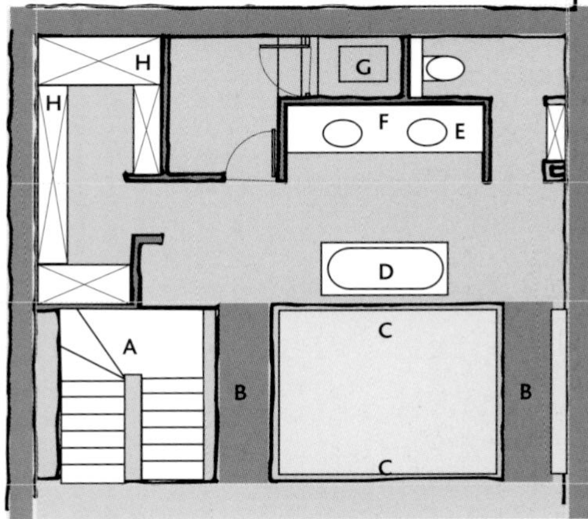

***This page*** In years of walking into peple's homes, this is the first time I have seen mirrors concealed behind doors that close flush to the wall. Not only does this device completely alter the focal point of a room by taking away the view of oneself in the mirror on entry, but it extends the eye away from the lengthier wall towards the window, the real focal point. Carmelite teaching stresses a moment when Tacitus encountered an altar erected without temple or image, *tantum ara et reverentia*. This bathroom is the same. Perhaps that is why it made me think of the Brittany order.

CASE STUDY | 4

**seamlessness** *There is a convent in Brittany near Dinan, the Abbaye de Boquen, whose gardens Proust called "the most silent place on Earth". It has white walls, in and out, and symmetrical simplicity of style. The Carmelite nuns, in off-white habits, are not allowed to speak: prayers are sung.*

**Light diffuses remarkably beautifully** through the convent windows, which contain plain rather than stained glass. The reason takes an eagle eye to detect: masses of linen fibres have been added to the glass during production, forming a sort of translucent matting inside it – a perfect and homegrown device (this is linen country) to bring good light play to the interior. The graceful trip through the convent is a thoroughly cleansing experience; the nuns even sell homegrown, additive-free bathroom products.

When I walked into the bathroom created by Vincent Van Duysen for his clients in Brussels (for the rest of the apartment, see pages 36–7 and 52–3), I was reminded of the Carmelite nuns' silent order. This bathroom is near perfection: a cathedral experience. Its light is very different morning and evening – in the evening it is particularly cool, almost blue, due to the northerly aspect. The room is vast and long, containing only light and bath, the latter almost altarlike in its prominence.

***Above*** Bathroom accoutrements are the new jewellery, their mechanisms cleverer and more concealed than ever. These taps and nozzle are the minimum required. Mixer taps are essential for water control.

***Left*** The freestanding bath is complete in its unornamented simplicity. Along an entire wall of the long bathroom is a unit with trough basins, his and hers, of Carrara marble. Floors and walls throughout the home are pure white marble, with scant veining.

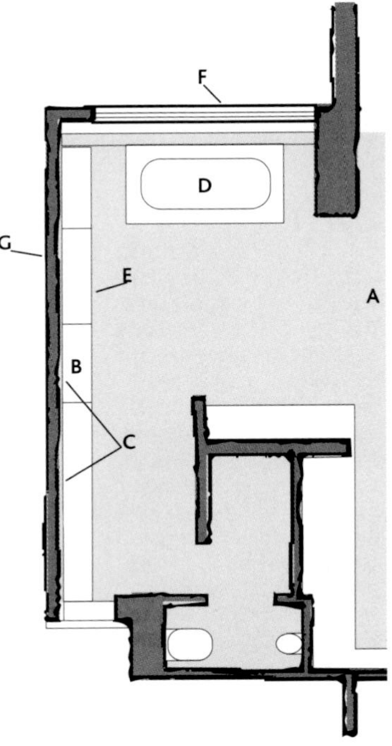


**A** Entry from dressing room
**B** Elongated marble double-trough basin
**C** Concealed mirrors
**D** Freestanding marble bath
**E** Pale-grey lacquered wood cabinetry
**F** Electronic light-diffusing blinds
**G** Marble walls

# solidity

*Susanna Colleoni's bathroom in Milan creates a wonderfully textured yet solid effect, largely through a technique of applying strips of marble to one of its walls. This is an elegant room, a bathroom that works for its attention to the placing of all elements, as well as materials used.*

**I remember the first time** I was particularly impressed in the building world: looking at a friend's swimming pool on Long Island, I realised the pattern of the pool's interior wall had been created by setting almost-metre-wide slabs of slate, one on top of another, all around and as deep as the pool. Thus a metre of pool wall would have taken probably twenty slabs of slate to create. The pool happens to be the most exquisite I have come across, its almost-black lining twinkling in the the light the sun pours onto the pool, but what extravagance, solidity and permanence.

So it is with equal interest that I view Susanna Colleoni's Milanese bathroom (for the rest of the house, see pages 20–3), for the technique used to produce her bathroom walls – the result is similar to the slate pattern of the Long Island pool. Covered with hand-

***Right and far right*** The bathroom furnishings are all by Boffi, including the wenge shelf that supports the washbasin. The bath is suspended in a light wood surround that stretches seamlessly the length of the wall. This wall, running alongside the bath and its support, appears layered horizontally, although in fact it is covered with strips of marble. The rough marble edges make a textured result: an onerous way to lay tiles, but worth the effort.

cut strips of marble, the wall behind the bath was influenced by the decoration of the Felsen-Therme spa in Vals, Switzerland. Only one wall is textured, but the mirror on an adjacent wall reflects the pattern of the slabs. I love the way the textured wall is cut down by the crispness of its neighbour. The effect in Colleoni's bathroom assists the horizontal plane in the room, in keeping with the popularity of width rather than height these days. Flat tiles would give the opposite effect, a vertical plane.

It is not until you scrutinise that you become aware of the attention to detail with which this bathroom has been honoured. The wooden floor, treated with a waterproof varnish to give it a pale milky finish, has a marble border. In the shower cubicle, the flooring has a more defined texture. The bathroom's myriad of creams and neutral tones is punctuated by the dark landscape of the wenge cantilevered shelf. The taps are set into the wall, all pipes hidden; it is as if the wall gives forth the water. This is a bathroom I would be happy to emulate in my own home.

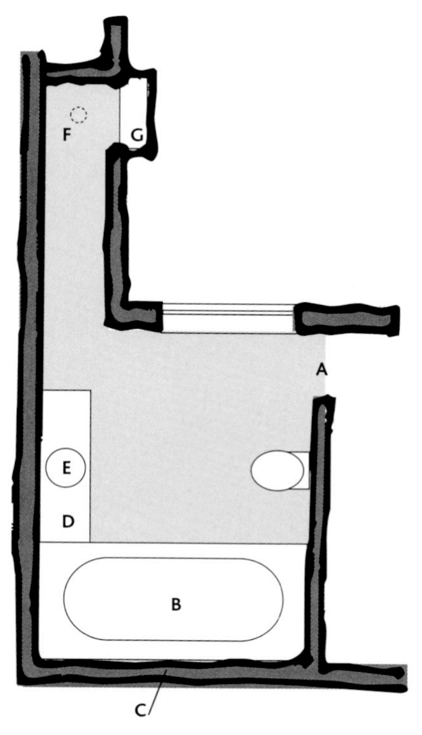


**A** Entry from bedroom
**B** Bath and bench surround
**C** Hand-cut marble-strip wall
**D** Cantilevered wenge-wood shelf
**E** Stone basin
**F** Shower room
**G** Shower-room seat in niche

***Above*** The large stone basin appears to be set into the thick, dark wood countertop, but in fact, the rounded underneath of the basin seen here is purely cosmetic, to conceal the outflow pipes. The bowl from this angle looks like a continuous whole; from above it can be seen to be flat-bottomed.

***Right*** In the slim shower cubicle, which is doorless, the stone theme continues. The shower dome is ceiling fitted, its pipes and mechanisms concealed.

# FUNCTIONAL | detail

# surfaces

Surfaces are key to the modern home, whether they are floor, wall or furniture surfaces. Good-looking and lasting interiors no longer depend on addition of mouldings, dados and frescoes; most architects and designers today believe the simpler the better. I tend to agree on the whole, although I think there is room for decorative detail if it enhances the room's overall atmosphere, or gives focal point to a room that is otherwise directionless. Stucco, simpler plaster techniques and concrete make for an extremely modern finish, where shadow gaps can become the "decorative" detail, but wallpapers, decorative paint effects and fabric-lined walls do not inhibit contemporary style. On the contrary, when cleverly applied, they can seem, in the twenty-first century, more contemporary than the above-mentioned finishes used in interiors since the mid-1950s, when Modernism had its heyday.

Whatever your choice, your surfaces can have a significant effect on your personal life, and even come to represent you. The point is illustrated by a tale of two houses.

The Farnsworth House (1945–51) by Mies van der Rohe stands in a meadow by the Fox River, west of Chicago. It was built for Dr Edith Farnsworth, an unmarried, financially secure nephrologist in her forties, embodying her architect's dictum "less is more": eight slender columns of white-painted steel support a transparent glass rectangular box; two horizontal planes, neat parallel bands of steel, hover above the ground as floor and roof. Inside, one large room is subdivided by a freestanding wooden core enclosing two bathrooms, a galley kitchen and a fireplace, the living areas otherwise open and unbounded.

Planning the house, Mies had said, "... here where everything is beautiful and privacy is not issue, it would be a pity to erect an opaque wall between the outside and the inside.... If we were building in the city or in the suburbs... I would make it opaque from outside and bring in the light through a courtyard garden in the middle." But he had not taken into account Farnsworth's conformism. She placed heirloom antique chairs in the dining room and Fu dogs on the terrace, but locals still saw the house as "like a tuberculosis sanatorium". In the 1970s she moved on, bitter at having been a nonconformist object of scrutiny.

Inspired by the Farnsworth House, architect Philip Johnson's Glass House in New Canaan, Connecticut, was built in 1949. Its floor is at ground level, screened by a hilly landscape. Johnson's design vocabulary is sophisticated . The cylindrical brick chimney echoes the traditional American family home, and the floor is a diagonal "brick" pattern, but that is where sentiment ends. However, linked to the glass space by a pathway is a windowless brick bunker of a "guest house", a defensible space of intimacy – the contrasting spaces of the two houses an essay on the overt and hidden sides of domestic life.

In 1993, asked about his Glass House as "a form of exhibitionism", Johnson responsed, "much more important than exhibitionism is the interface of architecture.... Whether you want to close yourself in is Freudian in one way, but exposing yourself is Freudian in another way." Solid or transparent, surfaces are much more than a mere backdrop.

# walls

Building walls requires thought, not only about style but also about their role in a coherent infrastructure. As architectural commentator Toshio Nakamura points out, construction "should be consistent and coherent from planning to detailing, in keeping with the hierarchical order and consecutive nature of the processes". If not, "the result will be ambiguous imagery of the whole, volatile profile of structure and prominent isolation of details."

With structure decided, which material should be used? Brick, concrete or wooden walls are characterised by their surface; glass walls by depth. Glass is an interesting option, altering the role of walls. Both reflective and transparent, it makes clear distinction between outside and inside, but eliminates the definitive boundary and seclusion. Glass walls define space but do not enclose it, dismissing the historical view that architecture should have internal and external space, interior and exterior profile.

Contemporary architects strive toward a flow of space within domestic interiors by removing internal walls. Favoured rooms are long expanses, uninterrupted by openings and space-inhibiting walls. Load-bearing internal walls are replaced by modern rafters (known as reinforced steel joists or RSJs) which dissect ceilings. Additional space created by opening up of rooms has meant greater exploration in dividing them using more shapely and appropriate walls, making the rooms' footprint more flexible. It is predicted that buildings of the future will be membranes that slide into load-bearing frameworks, varying space according to need. I have just seen an example of holiday homes using this technique, to be constructed in Devon.

LEONARDO DA VINCI
HAVANA

# inserting walls

Steel frames, able to span a large distance without support, mean walls can be removed or created at whim, allowing maximum use of the fourth architectural dimension: light. Light highlights walls and reduces their apparent mass and volume.

Use of glass has also changed since the advent of new techniques that enable it to become opaque or translucent at the flick of a switch, although for many translucent walls, in some countries at least, parchment or membrane remain in vogue. Japanese architect Tadao Ando goes so far as to create an adaptation of shoji (sliding panels, tradionally made from translucent paper in wooden frames, which can serve as walls or doors) out of poured concrete: bare concrete studded with holes against which sun strikes.

***Opposite and previous page*** Not only does glass take the inside of this Bel Air house out, but further spatial play is created by solid exterior walls which appear to strike through the glass, quite physically bringing the outdoors in.

***This page, top left*** In a London bathroom, a floating wall, mirrored on every face, reapportions space, maximises light and supports basin and vanity unit. Floating walls subdivide spaces and act as substantial yet decorative sculptural additions.

***Top right*** Here, in the Hollywood Hills, Japanese-style sliding shoji screens serve as closet doors, although they appear to be permanent paper walls.

***Bottom left*** In Milan, an *enfilade* of rooms (hallway, kitchen, dining area) is subdivided using smoothly pivoting glass doors that allow light to flow and help create an axis and feeling of fluidity from room to room.

***Bottom right*** This Manhattan apartment is a simple white space, with two walls between sitting room and dining room constructed to produce a minimal galley kitchen. Wall finishes throughout are the same white matte paint.

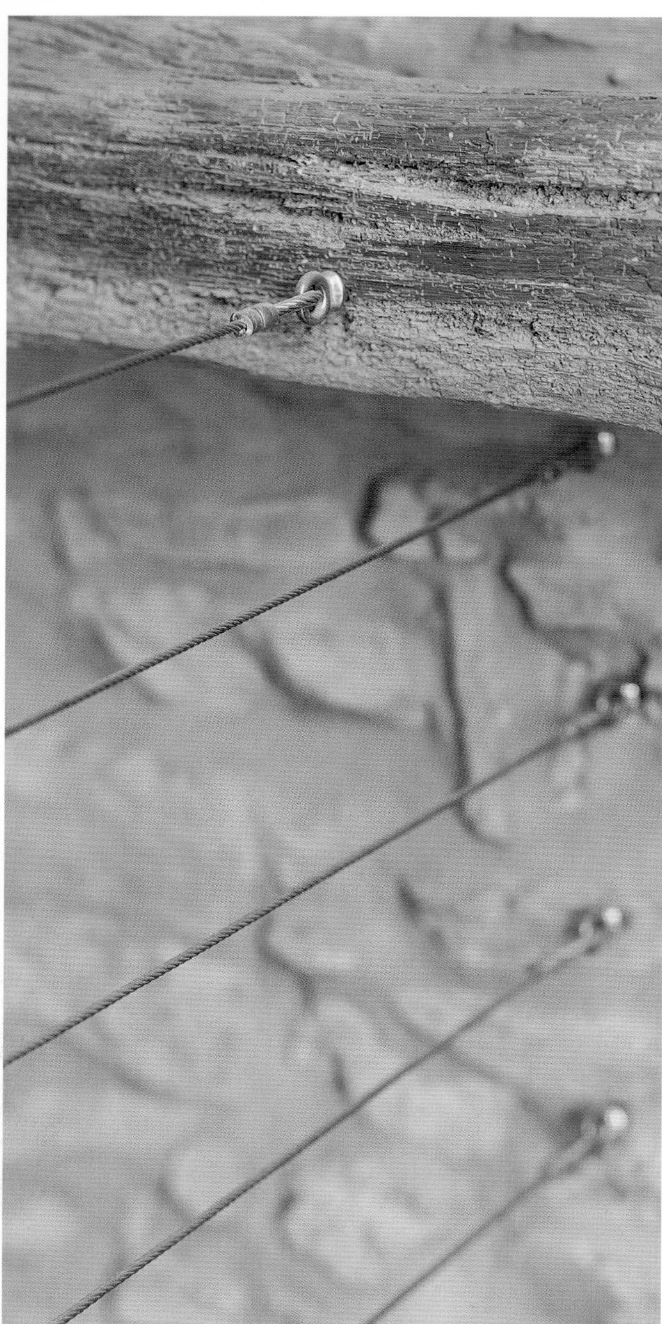

***Left*** Belgian farm buildings, turned into a family home, retain much of the shell, yet many levels have been built within the space, with addition of staircases and walkways. Steel wires fixed to original walls and beams secure safety.

***Right, top*** At the other end of the same farmhouse, random stone interior walls remain exposed, the contemporary staircase a reminder of today. If leaving walls exposed, check that mortar is in good condition or you will have to point it: a clear sealer on new brick or stone walls will stop them from crumbling or becoming a dust trap.

***Right, bottom*** Quaker Barn is a converted nineteenth-century single-storey farm building in East Anglia. Architect Anthony Hudson installed an internal knapped flint wall, a local material found within five miles of the barn, to separate open-plan living from sleeping quarters. Glass pantiles draw light in.

***Opposite*** A truly eclectic room with origins east and west: the red chairs and cushions seem Chinese influenced, the ottoman a Miesian inflection. The walls are indisputably taken from Japan: perforated concrete slabs are a signature of Japanese architect Tadao Ando, although he does not own the concept of bare cast concrete as interior option.

# bare walls

Mankind has been building with brick for over five thousand years, using local clay to make standardised units resistant to fire, decay and weather. While stone requires laborious cutting and handling, brick is small enough to hold in one hand, freeing the other for a trowel. Bricks add character. From the chimneys of Hampton Court near London to the apse of St Fosca's church in Venice, they have been widely used. Architect Mario Botta favours their use in the modern world – for instance in San Francisco's new art museum.

Exposing brick, stone or concrete gives a nod to a building's roots, in terms of whereabouts or function. Locally quarried stone may be exposed in a rural English home, brick or concrete left bare in ex-industrial spaces. I cannot quite accept the use of breeze block for interior walls, but I love concrete, exposed brick and stone walls, and I predict their re-entry into the most fashionable of homes.

# cladding

Interior wood cladding is popular with traditionalists and modernists alike: it is sumptuous but demure, the sable lining to a fur coat. Oak panelling speaks of substance and history; the first in Scotland was put into Edinburgh Castle around 1605. In ordinary houses hardwood is rare, but softwood is quite common, if not wholly attractive, on ceilings or under dado rails.

In application and sentiment, wood interiors reflect the times. Greene and Greene's 1907–9 David B. Gamble house in Pasadena, California, was teak clad. The flat-roofed Villa Muller by Adolf Loos in Prague (1928–30) incorporated wood cladding, as did the penthouse by Russian emigré Berthold Lubetkin at Highpoint 2 in north London. There it was fir wood. More recently, Berlin's New Art Gallery (1992–8) was oak lined by Hilmer & Sattler, as was Jil Sander's Tokyo store (Elisabeth Boesch and Martin Boesch). Wood is a very chic choice indeed.

Effects can vary greatly: light timbers such as sycamore look and feel very different to tongue-and-groove cladding in oak. Modular wood wall and ceiling panels can be positioned to influence room proportions. The company Poliform produces splendid modular wall-to-wall furniture of solid wood and wood veneer.

Cladding can mean a lining of other materials too, of course – marble, metal, stone, travertine, plaster: just about any material. Metal cladding is better when used discerningly, and not all over.

***Opposite, top left*** Ready-cut and finished panels of plywood can simulate anything from weathered cypress to wormy chestnut. Eric Gizard in Paris has chosen a strong grain for his bedroom.

***Opposite, top right*** In Mark Rios's bedroom in Bel Air, California, the eye is drawn by the single wall of tongue-and-groove taupe-painted boards. If more walls had been clad, the room would seem cramped.

***Opposite, bottom*** This entire Brussels apartment is clad in marble, much too expensive for most people's means. The "shadow gap" lifts the feeling of weight, making the effect more serene, and helps define the all-white space.

***Above left*** Here light oak lines a wall, and a solid-oak, floor-to-ceiling pivoting door (with exquisite action) makes it appear seamless. A delightful combination of contemporary and traditional fireplace in this Paris home.

***Above*** Shelton and Mindel's upstate New York client hand-picked the trees, then the timber, for her panelling, seeking almost identical graining as well as tone. The result is splendid, both poetic and prosaic.

***Left*** Wall treatment can set a mood. Jasper Conran's London bathroom, with tongue-and-groove dove-coloured painted planks, is East Hampton country chic, but just as at home in London. It evokes simple, subtle luxury.

# tile

Dating back to 5000 BC, tile was used by Egyptian pharaohs in their tombs; Roman mosaics are tiles too. By about AD 1100, many European countries were making ceramic tile, expensive and largely for religious orders. In a hot climate tiles are invaluable: ancient and modern North Africa is full of them, and they are widely used in Spain, Portugal and Italy, while Venezuela and Brazil have set trends in their use on walls as space dividers.

In temperate climates tiles are often best left to the bathroom, and sometimes the kitchen, although today we have fantastic kitchen alternatives. Grouting is easier to keep clean in the more sterile bathroom than in a kitchen. Mirrored, glass and stone are preferable to ceramic, which is less durable. When it is impractical to use slabs of stone or slate, stone tiles make a good alternative. Mosaics can be tricky if elaborate, although young designer Fabio Novembre has worked wonders with mosaic tiles from Bisazza.

One tiled wall may suffice a contemporary scheme. Three walls can be spectacular with a fourth of contrasting texture. Slate, stone and glass benefit from colour or tone mix (because within them are many tones), but ceramic tiles do not. Tiles are either all right or all wrong. Choose carefully: unlike paint, tile cannot readily be altered.

***Far left, above*** Ceramic tiles offer a wide choice of colours, glazes, patterns and textures. I prefer them glossy, if not glassy.

***Far left, below*** The tiles are hand-cut Carrara marble, hard wearing and impervious to staining. True marble is the ultimate, but precast composites of marble chips bonded with resin are less expensive. Small marble tiles should be real marble and hand-cut.

***Left*** A wall between shower and bathroom is made from semi-opaque glass brick, an invention that has dated quickly. Used sensibly, however, it combines privacy and light.

***Right*** Stone is waterproof and easy to clean. Here, large brownish Indian slate tiles contrast with colourful smaller "mosaic" tiles. Slate is a dense non-porous stone which varies in colour. It always looks good in square or rectangular form.

***Right*** A dark greenish-black matte wall is backdrop to a Paris fabric collection. In eighteenth-century Europe, greys were fashionable. Under Victorian influence, dark hues, mauve, taupe and brown were the mode. Later came pastels, bubblegum brights and safe beige. The brave find dark colours can create an intense mood. Dark rooms look small but interesting; I'd say, paint a small room a dark colour but let a large room breathe.

***Opposite, top left*** John Stedila designed his own lacquer screen in teal blue, a sophisticated shade; the settee is eighteenth-century French. Accent colour need not be pin-pricks: it can take up a substantial proportion of a room otherwise garbed in neutral hues. Here the ceiling is extremely high and the screen anchors this side of the room. Gloss and glazed walls offer reflection.

***Opposite, top right*** This Manhattan home uses bright and unusual colours successfully. Pinks usually look good when there is a little creamy yellow to point them up. This bluish pink helps to bring out the blue of the art. Study colour theory a little before making decisions, to maximise the effects of different colours.

***Opposite, bottom*** It is odd how many fashion designers end up wearing black. The Manhattan dining room of gown designers Mark Badgley and James Mischka is painted "espresso" – it took four coats – a black-and-white theme echoed in the photographs by Claire Flanders. The rock-crystal chandelier serves as jewellery. The chairs are1940s by Jens Risom.

## colour

I am always fascinated by how things came about. Wall paint is one the most enduring elements since man first walked our planet: drawings in Palaeolithic caves lead to the belief that paint must be at least fifty thousand years old. Beginning as pure pigment, paint is now a scientific combination of pigment, solvents and thinners.

At one time, colours were limited to primary hues. Later, when dyes were invented, paint took on many variations in colour. Today we tend to use multiple neutral or monotone shades, against which we play jabs of accent colour. Light and texture play an enormous part: no colour looks the same under different lights and when textures change.

As a wall covering, paint has many practical advantages. It helps seal the walls and keeps moisture from seeping through. It is relatively inexpensive and easy to apply (a survey suggests that in the United States over seventy percent of home owners apply their own paint).

# pattern

It used to be thought that decorative wallpaper was an invention of the Chinese, but there is little evidence to show that it was present in the Far East any earlier than in Europe: it is believed Louis XI was the first monarch to place an order for wallpaper. In a English publication dated 1699, it is stated that in Surrey, paperhangings (an early word for wallpaper) were sometimes known as "paper tapistry" (*sic*), and this description aptly fitted a practical and cheap substitute for the costly decorative hangings favoured by the wealthy. Even at this date, paper was sold in rolls. Wallpaper was first regarded as a substitute for tapestry, painted cloths, leather and wood panelling, and possibly it is still a substitute for modern wall finishes.

Now, however, it is not wallpaper we question, but its pattern. I do not think wallpaper or murals should be sniffed at. They can add great depth to a room which has relatively few other redeeming features. Architectural rooms are seen as multifaceted sculpture, plainly decorated homes (perhaps with painted or textured walls) as abstract art, and the patterned room as a collage.

***Opposite, top left*** Pattern should be considered as art for the home, and is often a giveaway to period. Fine decorative paintwork – *faux bois*, *faux marbre* and so on – is a good alternative to heavy woods and stones, but wallpaper, here "Kew" by Jocelyn Warner, is an easier form of decoration.

***Opposite, top right*** All walls of this bedroom are covered in egg-pattern wallpaper ("Totem", also by Warner), adding to the spatial quality. Large-patterned papers are better in subtle shades; here, furniture has been scaled up so it does not fall into oblivion.

***Opposite, bottom left*** Stripes give a room height, if of the right width, and work well in a symmetrical room. Striped wallpaper can replace painted stripes, although paint adds texture.

***Opposite, bottom right*** Wallpaper seems less acceptable in downstairs rooms, such as this basement dining room, but it works here thanks to the lack of clutter and because its design (again Warner) is geometric and unfussy.

***Above*** Wallpaper, here Warner's "Larger Than Life" lily motif, can set a room's pace. First choose a paper you find pleasing, then key fabrics and carpet to it. You will like fewer wallpapers, so if at all possible don't choose flooring first.

***Right*** A patterned ceiling will always seem lower, but can be splendid. This one, by Eric Gizard, is meant to be seen, as part of the art collection within: it was commissioned by artist David Tremlett. The ceiling-suspended lights are by Pierre Scholtes, the chairs by Souplina.

# floors

Long ago, the lower horizontal surfaces of a room were simply tamped or beaten-down earth, covered with skins or textiles. We still tend to create a floor surface then, depending on the climate, add "skin" for warmth or protection (of feet or floor finish).

Later, stone pavings were introduced, and in Roman times cement and terrazzo – small pieces of marble embedded in cement – became common, as well as the better-known mosaic (often richly patterned) and marble (just rich). Perhaps the most primitive mosaics came from New Guinea: trophy skulls and masks covered with rows of small shells. In the Neolithic period, floors of water-worn pebbles were laid in Crete, and it was Aegean culture that supplied the first mosaics. As these were created for floors, they needed to last and be relatively flat: mosaic seems to have developed not as multiple pieces of inlay but from differential treatment of surfaces for magical potency, enrichment and decoration. In the Middle Ages use of tiled floors spread; they were the rule in all great churches, where we find evidence of much design history.

Wooden floors also appeared early, especially in domestic work and buildings of more than one storey. Nowadays, wooden floors have two layers; in previous centuries they were sometimes single.

Floors are a matter of taste, but must also be up to their traffic. Who would have thought that humble concrete, used by the Romans for aqueducts and bridges, would be an elegant choice for flooring today? Yet it has a cool and calm nature, invaluable in a turbulent world. Rugs and carpets are not to be scoffed at, but are really just a decorative wrap, a bit of colour or warmth. The simplest of floors can be beautiful, a layering in an expanse of space.

***Opposite*** Clear or pigmented epoxy binders can be fused with multi-coloured or natural stone, sometimes quartz for a dazzling effect; this one is marble and resin. Many such floors are fast-curing and unaffected by sunlight, which makes them popular for outdoor use too.

***Previous page*** The flooring is seamless with the walls, all faces marble. (Marble is porous, so stains must be wiped immediately.) Van Duysen's ultimate minimal environment gives a nod to the senior master of the craft, John Pawson, whose bowl takes centre stage.

***Left*** White resin with powdered mother-of-pearl for a "champagne" swirling effect has been poured over a living-room floor for a luxurious, clean look. Quality resins are the key components in most composite flooring.

***Left, below*** Always consult a professional when laying terrazzo. In this 1860s New York townhouse, the floor is supported by steel posts in the basement. Terrazzo is suitable for underfloor heating, but can be hard and noisy. Marble and terrazzo should not be sealed because finishes can be destroyed.

# composite

One of the most effective ways to present a floor is by pouring it: there are fantastic floors created using poured resin and composites, and concrete, made essentially from stone and gravel, is poured too. Resin floors are durable, seamless, skid-resistant, chemical-resistant and excellent for domestic and commercial space, and come in just about any colour. Epoxy is one type of resin, methacrylate another. The latter is a new poured seamless flooring with an incredibly short cure time of only an hour, despite being applied at cold temperatures; it is highly impact-resistant and can be applied to concrete or steel. Both epoxy and methacrylate impart a high-gloss but low-glare satin or flat finish. Poured floors seem to be the modern way forward, although prices vary enormously: flooring remains one of the largest expenses in a house.

Some composites, bonded but not poured, offer an alternative to solid wood floors. Particle board (or chipboard), made from wood chips bonded in a resin, is famously pocket-saving and can be attractive, either sealed or unsealed.

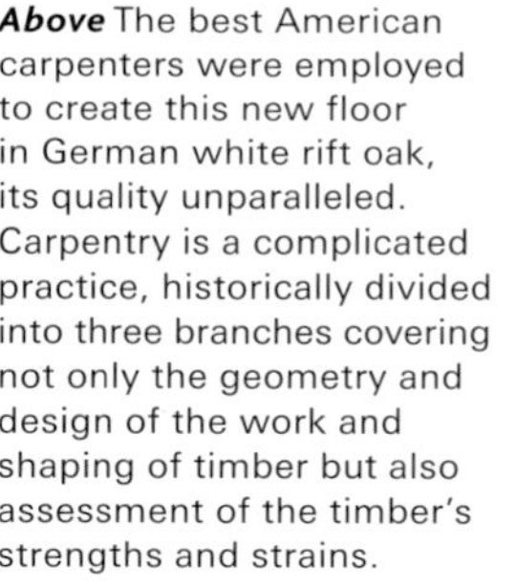

***Above*** The best American carpenters were employed to create this new floor in German white rift oak, its quality unparalleled. Carpentry is a complicated practice, historically divided into three branches covering not only the geometry and design of the work and shaping of timber but also assessment of the timber's strengths and strains.

***Above*** Geometric pattern on wooden flooring, produced by staining or a mix of materials (wood and slate, for example), can be stunning. This is custom produced, but companies such as the Dutch Rowi produce parquet that emulates the touch of the hand in many woods, from Canadian hard maple to teak and even bamboo.

***Above*** In a scheme by French designer Frédéric Méchiche, an existing floor has been stripped back, sanded, stained and treated. If your existing floor is in good condition, it can be sanded and sealed. In newer houses boards may be tongue-and-grooved, while in older houses they are more likely to be butt-jointed.

***Above*** This pristine expanse of floor in stained oak is a major part of the home's visual layering. You can always tell the rough from the smooth, professional sanding (the product of six weeks' intensive training) from amateur work. Since we tend not to cover floors these days with rugs, it makes sense to go the added mile.

## wood

Traditional and popular, wooden floors are often made from oak, beech, ash or birch (although beech, as tough as nails, is hard to sand and its pores are too small for staining). Other good choices include American black cherry: a beautiful colour, it is more dent-resistant than birch but softer than oak.

Wooden floors must be sealed; unsealed wood is not waterproof or greaseproof and is likely to stain. Softer woods (such as pine – sometimes attractive in the country, but generally rather too hippy for my taste) require more sealer. Some varnishes and lacquers are suitable for wooden floors, but are not as durable. Most sealers have a gloss finish, but some are semi-gloss or matte and preserve the wood's natural appearance. Any seal changes the colour slightly, oleo-resinous ones tending to darken more in time. Oleo-resinous seals

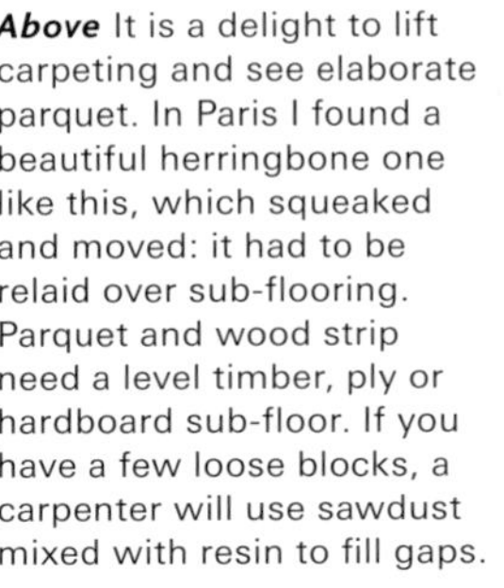

***Above*** It is a delight to lift carpeting and see elaborate parquet. In Paris I found a beautiful herringbone one like this, which squeaked and moved: it had to be relaid over sub-flooring. Parquet and wood strip need a level timber, ply or hardboard sub-floor. If you have a few loose blocks, a carpenter will use sawdust mixed with resin to fill gaps.

***Above*** Jasper Conran's floor is oak. White oak is a favourite of the profession: in a rift or quarter-sawn shade, it shows off medullar rays like no other wood, and is more moisture-stable than red oak. Among many good options for flooring is Jotoba or Brazilian cherry; harder than American cherry, it is difficult to obtain but worth the effort and expense.

***Above*** Start by calling in a wood specialist to assess damage and advise you whether to relay or start again. If your existing floor is very uneven, explore possible causes before embarking on restoration. You might have damp, a leaking pipe, or structural movement. This floor has undergone some restoration but retains its charm.

***Above*** A painted wooden floor can work well in a relaxed country or seaside environment but, to my mind, looks somewhat temporary or studenty in town, unless in pristine white. Any gloss paint can be used, although specially produced floor paints are much better for application and durability (yacht paint is particularly hard-wearing).

partly soak into the wood grain and move with the wood, while polyurethane seals form a hard surface skin which may not be appropriate for new wood floors, as they tend to shrink, cracking the finish.

Stained floors are very respectable – floor stains are available in wood tones and colours, but the latter can be tying and tend to date. There are various water-based and spirit-based stains (the latter contain oil), and chemical dyes too. If applying sealer to a stained floor, ensure the sealer is compatible with the stain, particularly if the stain contains oil. Water-based stain can be sealed without chemical reaction, so if you are attempting the project alone, it might be best to stick with this and avoid a nasty glutinous mess. Floors should be sanded smooth before staining, because staining will raise the grain.

# stone

Stone is lovely, and even better if indigenous, although marble is generally imported. Often a local quarry gives the best colours for the area, or at least reminds us of its colours. Furthermore, local stone will be suited to climatic conditions. This said, there are some wonderful stones becoming available for export: Kirkstone is a pale sea-green volcanic stone from the Lake District in England that has become quarriable thanks to new diamond-cutting techniques. Some volcanic stones have been somewhat oversold due to fad, and be careful of the volcanic tuft Canterra and Adoquin for wet areas: they do not perform well in swimming pools or bathrooms.

Stone comes in many finishes with technical names – bushammered, hammer-dressed, polished, rubbed, honed, striated – each with its own look. And for real stone fanatics, there's the autumn marble fair at Verona in Italy.

***Right*** Geometry plays a part in creation of hard flooring. Stone is cut to form shapes that must not detract from the rest of the room; concrete screed can be moulded into almost any shape but must be scored to prevent random cracking.

***Far right*** This old stone floor is original to the Belgian farmhouse. A honed (abraded) finish has better coefficient of friction than a polished one. Mixing stones that can and cannot be polished brings a longterm maintenance problem; better to mix textures.

***Right, below*** A seating area comprises a recessed table and resilient Brazilian Rio Verde slate floor, with cushions leather-covered for warmth and durability.

***Far right, below*** All slates (this, in Los Angeles, is from India) and sandstones are not equal, and should not be used without advice in areas that are frequently wet; nor should polished, slippery floors, or inferior marble that may crack. With slate, look for "I" for interior use or "E" for exterior.

***Opposite*** For real terrazzo, as here, a fine marble-chip mixture that may be colour-pigmented is blended and placed on a concrete foundation. Additional colours can be tossed in, then a lightweight roller is used. When dry, a heavy grinder "polishes" the surface, followed by hand trowelling before cleaning, polishing and sealing.

***This page*** Optical carpets and those with geometric designs have been seen for centuries. Today, with technological advancement, complicated designs are becoming more and more simple to define. Architect Eric Gizard in Paris, a relative newcomer, designs his own optical collection; this carpet is called "Tarkett Sommer". Its principal graphic, a computer-generated image, is a trompe l'oeil bubble.

***Opposite, top left*** Felting is the most ancient of carpet techniques. The earliest known whole specimen is third or fourth century BC: a rectangle of black wool, or possibly hair felt, with a white border along one side, to which silhouettes of feline heads in red or blue are appliquéd with split stitch. This rug, while less ornamental, seems both ancient and modern.

***Opposite, top right*** The circular rug acts as an island in a square room, and helps to unite the scheme so that the secondary living room does not become a corridor. Lee Mindel commissions custom rugs from the masterly V'Soske Joyce Ltd, of the Republic of Ireland, who use the finest of linens, silks and wools and work with the best colour palettes.

***Opposite, bottom left*** The Japanese were the pioneers of modular building: all timber sizes are determined by the *tatami* mat-sizing procedure, thus Japanese houses are designed around standard-size mats. Sisal is the nearest Western material to *tatami* (which is made of soft reed): although not constructed in the same manner, it has a natural, stretched feel to it. *Tatami* absorbs moisture and apparently has health benefits thanks to its soothing smell.

# soft floors

When we want a little comfort, or an island around which to centre a room, a touch of softness, a rug, can be the answer, and can unify a colour scheme. Many rugs have a multitude of colours in them that are not all visible to the eye but can tie other elements together.

Wall-to-wall carpets can be smart too; some of my all-time loves were designed by David Hicks in the 1960s and made by Avina carpets. I lived with acres of a hexagonal design of his in a friend's Sloane Square apartment many years ago, and have been reminded of its effect by very graphical, well-designed websites whose visuals sweep you up and plunge you forward.

The prime advantage to carpets and rugs is as sound absorber, the second to add physical warmth and perhaps surprise. In the New York apartment of architect Christopher Smallwood, I was surprised to find lovely blue-and-white striped Indian dhurries protecting more exotic rugs underneath. I think rugs should be walked on and the patina of time should either never happen (if the rug is ultra-durable) or happen with aplomb. High-traffic areas need the best quality, but why stop there?

# structure

The late-nineteenth-century novelist Edith Wharton was an individual way ahead of her time. Apart from being the first woman to win the Pulitzer Prize, she was closely associated with the birth of interior design in the United States, inspired by the work of Beaux-Arts architects Charles McKim and Stanford White, and preached cautious, sensible good taste for the home. For Wharton, a study of the house plan, including all elevations, and of any detailed architectural renderings, was to be made before room design began. This must have taken hours of laborious drawing, but was worthwhile. With computer-aided imaging, it has become easier and more accurate, and there are companies specialising in assisting with such drawings for professionals and innocents alike. These drawings can then be used when deciding upon furniture scale and placement (the pieces can be modelled in: there are firms which supply, as a promotional tool, computer-drawn 3D models of modern classics, furniture, lamps and so on, anything you can find in a store, to download into your virtual space). You can even order a virtual tour of your intended home, and play with the surfaces in it to boot. Good interior designers and certainly architects will offer this service as routine.

Proportion leading to harmony was Wharton's key principle of interior decoration, and she revealed the important elements of a room in her famed manual *The Decoration of Houses*, published in collaboration with Ogden Codman, Jr in 1897, very specifically to be walls, doors, ceilings, floors and, last but not least, windows: "Not only do they represent the three chief essentials of its [a room's] comfort – light, heat and means of access – but they are the leading features in that combination of voids and masses that forms the basis of architectural harmony." What prescience for a woman who lived in the late Victorian period, when bric-a-brac seemed to rule most people's aesthetic vision for the home. The fashionable contemporary home may have neither interior doors nor stairs (bungalow is a word misunderstood, which I think should be brought back into everyday use: it is an Anglo-Indian term, taken from the vernacular for a typical single storey-home lived in by Europeans in India), but if these elements are desired – doors for privacy, heat and sound insulation, stairs to lead from one floor to another – then planning is essential. I have seen many inner-city homes recently where an elevator is installed and stairwells used backstage only for health and safety. Elevators can be space-saving in a large home but take more space than imagined in a smaller home because of the mechanics required; elevator additions in many Parisian buildings rarely have room for a handbag, let alone luggage, when occupied by two people.

Oscar Wilde, another eminent Victorian (he lived until 1900), said that changes in opinion were typical of people who think. It can take much deliberation to find your preferred staircase, or to design the perfect spaces it sits within and connects or the doors and windows that make for smooth living. Think hard, change your mind as often as you like on the drawing board, again and again, then put a full stop to it.

# stairs

Before stairs were common, they embodied a resonant symbolism of gradation and ascension (religious or otherwise), notably between this world and spirit realms. Today staircases can be trouble, the legalities a quagmire: it is essential to consult relevant building regulations to ascertain legal requirements, or you may be ascending to the spirit world before you realise your dreams! Materials must be fire-resistant and many countries regulate size.

Abetted by properties of materials like steel and glass, many contemporary staircases are the epitome of structural ingenuity and refinement (think Eva Jiricna and Richard Rogers). They may be the glittering jewels of commercial architecture, but for the home we need materials closer to our roots (please do not consider green glass: it is the least human material, rarely appropriate except in the most public of spaces). Concrete and wood are more satisfying and durable; concrete can be lovely, and good with underheated floors for an overall feeling of warmth. Steel has its place: it can be contorted into sinuous form, and staircases of steel, in a virtuoso performance, appear to almost float in space.

Top of the hit parade of staircases is the concrete design by Eero Saarinen for the General Motors Technical Center in Detroit, exploiting the potential of new technologies. Reinforced cast-concrete treads (cast separately) are suspended from steel tensile wires in what appears a dramatic balancing act.

***Above left*** Effective modern staircases are often cantilevered, or seemingly so (steps used to be embedded into the wall, but with new construction methods this is not always necessary). They occupy little space, and are wonderful for sight line. A cantilevered staircase without a handrail is usually legal domestically (verify this where you live), but not always recommended. Under no circumstances attempt to build a staircase without professional supervision.

***Above*** This spiral staircase fits snugly between wall and newel (helical stairs are spirals with no central post or newel, allowing light through the shaft). Spiral staircases should not be used for heights of more than 4 metres (13 feet) in a home, for comfort, and in some areas this is a legal limit. Although less space is taken up, more effort is required to climb spirals and they are considered less safe than conventional staircases, but are an option in a confined space.

***Right*** A freestanding staircase can be a sculptural component that acts as a focal point and takes up a significant proportion of a room. I feel this kind of statement is not often required in a home, although such staircases do have use in public spaces. This is a good home solution: the staircase appears freestanding but is attached at one side to the glass wall, behind which, in an inner courtyard, is a water feature that changes the direction of the room, making the staircase less dominant than the feature.

***Left*** Doors, windows and stairs punctuate the fluidity of a space, which helps create harmony: bad or illogical design can produce an aesthetic stammer or a breakdown in communication between rooms. Traditional staircases, like this in upstate New York, can be given a modern slant by simplifying what is around them. The arch of the two-storey-high window above the front door is reflected beautifully by the form of this staircase.

***Above*** The Egyptian deity Osiris was invoked as "he who stands at the top of the stairs" and the tops of stairs are as crucial as staircases themselves for house harmony. Here, a traditional banister has been replaced by a simple safety structure, like those copied by Modernist architects from ships.

***Above right*** An industrial-style staircase, resembling an exterior fire escape, coexists with ancient stone. Real industrial staircases are usually multi-flight, with rest areas, and predominate in public buildings where ceilings are high; unless you occupy a vast industrial space, you are unlikely to seek this option. This staircase looks simply hoisted into place but was very much considered.

***Right*** Single-flight staircases, where steps succeed each other uninterrupted, are the most utilised in the home. They are usually straight but can incorporate a change in direction. Wood and steel are preferred materials for their light weight. "Under the stairs" is now an outmoded term: these areas, once closets of clutter, no longer exist in the modern home.

***This page*** Half psychological screen, half insulation (mainly against sound), a pivoting floor-to-ceiling wooden door in Mark Rios's California home divides reception rooms (in the background) from bedroom and bathroom (foreground). A matching ceiling panel accesses a storage area.

***Right*** Handles and locks can make or break the finish of your home. This example is based on a Bauhaus-design cylindrical lever handle by Walter Gropius for the Fagus works in 1923: the first handle for mass production. The German-based Technoline firm is the main licensed maker of Bauhaus handles.

***Far right, top*** A top-hung sliding door disappears fully into a wall (the floor is unbroken) and this clever handle, flush to the wall, is the way to pull it out again. Sliding doors are graceful and ensure that valuable space is not wasted.

***Far right, bottom*** Doors, like windows, can be used to diffuse light. Architect Stephen Roberts utilises floor-to-ceiling hingeless doors with an ethereal quality as pauses between rooms. Two pairs of purpose-built interior steel-framed doors with white interlayer glass inhabit this relatively minimal space.

# doors & windows

Historically, doors in grander houses were built to reflect the importance of a room, and thus would vary in height from room to room. Before our current home, a skinny and tall Georgian house where symmetry abounds, we lived in a mansion-block apartment where, on entering the apartment, the three doors to the left, which announced the principal living rooms, were much taller than the three on the right, which led to the supporting rooms, the kitchen and so on. The effect really bothered me: it made me feel lopsided. A double door width is probably the best way to announce a very formal room, but otherwise I think doors should on the whole remain one height within an area of a home. Ceiling-height doors are lovely.

The door as we know it is surprisingly young. Doors started life as primitive sheets of hide or textiles which hung as flaps or rolled up. In the tomb of Ti, from fifth-dynasty Egypt, elaborate wall paintings represented doors of richly decorated matting which rolled to the top, like an awning, to admit entrance; in Italian churches to this day, flaps made from leather can be found as secondary doors. Egypt produced the first solid doors, and as today, these wooden doors were single boards (although they were heavier then), with pivots at the top

***Left*** Glass is a versatile material, and its surface effects can play a pragmatic role as well as being decorative. Sand-blasting, bead-blasting and acid-etching provide different solutions for keeping glass translucent but not wholly transparent, so that bathroom and basin areas behind surface-treated glass doors, as here, remain partially concealed. To the outsider, when the doors are closed, the soft-focus effect can be dreamy.

***Below*** Sliding flat doors depend upon wall space at the sides to accommodate them as they slide across or into the wall, like these in the apartment by Vincent Van Duysen. Sliding doors can disappear completely or flank the door opening on one side of the wall. The folding sliding door also exists, concertinaing together as it slides: its panels are generally hinged or secured together by a skin or covering.

***Right*** The advantage of a top-hung pivoting door is that it can be much wider than a side-hung door and has no frame. In glass, the door practically disappears; the yellow glass door to the study extension in this house in London's Notting Hill is an effective foil against noise and a colourful addition to an already colourful house. Its transparency discloses the rare furniture in the study, including a hinged-top desk by Jeannette Laverière.

and bottom of one side fitted into sockets in the sill and head. When the doorway was wide, two doors would be used, pivoted on the outside edges. Stone was used where wood was scarce, and would not have been the first choice but a necessity (Syria produced stone doors in the fourth to sixth centuries). There have been discoveries of doors from Augustan-era Rome in Pompeii, made of marble, panelled ingeniously to reduce the weight without lessening strength, form ever following function.

The doors we consider to be "country style" or rustic, built of several pieces, had their inception in warmer climates where wood would warp easily: they were built up of several pieces, either a series of planks tied with tenons, dowels or horizontal braces (known as battens), or alternatively by forming a framework of uprights stiles and horizontal members (the rails), with thinner panels between them held by grooves or additional mouldings. (In Syria, Palestine and Mesopotamia, wooden doors were often sheathed in sheets of richly repoussé metal, examples of which can be seen in London's British Museum.) Modern doors and their mechanisms for opening are as varied as the ancient, although in recent years especially they have become less and less ornate.

Windows were held in great esteem by Philip Larkin, the mid-twentieth-century English poet, a view concurrent with his time: "Rather than words comes the thought of high windows: The sun comprehending glass, And beyond it, the deep blue air, that shows Nothing, and is nowhere, and is endless."

The advent of sunbathing and a new interest in the outdoors precipitated larger windows in modern interiors: emphasis was upon making the interior lighter to reflect a healthy outlook on life. In Victorian times, sunlight had been thought harmful, windows a harbourer of bacteria, partly because in the great outdoors sickness was rife, and the nineteenth century in England saw window tax at its most peculiar, with city houses of over eight windows subject to a surcharge. Now nineteenth-century homes became less acceptable for their dust and fuss. Around 1930 window mania struck the architectural fraternity.

Apart from an increase in ratio of window to wall, simpler shapes became popular. Le Corbusier, in the late 1920s at the Villa Savoye outside Paris, created "ribbon" windows, horizontal wraparound affairs with small or medium-sized panes set around a building at waist height or just above. Then controversial "window wall" houses were built by Ludwig

***Opposite, top left*** Sliding shoji screens in California lead from hallway to kitchen. Shoji are translucent paper doors or windows – simple, functional and beautiful; the original Japanese shoji is a rice-paper screen in a sliding wooden frame, usually divided into panels.

***Opposite, top right*** This pivoting glass door in Milan, with its pivot point a third of the way along, is balanced so it stays open at 90 degrees. Totally glass doors in public places must have a sign on the glass to show it is there. In a home these are not necessary but accidents do occur. Pivoting doors must be unencumbered and can take up much space.

***Opposite, bottom left*** Paris has some tiny bathrooms. I was once renting a flat on rue Molière that actor Rupert Everett came to view: the rest of the apartment was palatial but he asked to see the cubicle, and sat for some minutes discussing the lack of leg room. Here, in Eric Gizard's Paris bathroom, meticulous planning and use of doors mean there is just enough room in lavatory (left door) and shower (right), yet the bathroom remains part of the open-plan scheme.

***Opposite, bottom right*** A house's character can be dramatically modernised by changing door proportions, in this case opening up a doorway to twice its former width. Modern doors vary in dimensions; in the eighteenth century it was held that height should be at least twice the width.

***Right, top*** This window leads to another window, and in between is a shower room. Natural light pours through; there is also artificial lighting for after dark. The window is needed in a dark corridor, the shower maximising space in this London house.

***Right*** Steel-framed doors to a New York bamboo garden, by Crittall, are the type used by Gropius and Lloyd Wright in the 1920s and 1930s. Two pairs of these doors are the only "windows" on this side.

Mies van der Rohe and Philip Johnson (see page 99) to let light in while keeping the elements out. These were followed by the work of Richard Neutra, who used glass for walls on inside exterior walls of L-shaped houses in Los Angeles, understanding the need for privacy.

For postwar twentieth-century folk, multiple large windows became a symbol of newfound freedom. As late as 1959 the first decent length of glass, over three metres (eleven feet) and capable of being lifted to building sites, was poured from a furnace in England.

Glass has evolved enormously in recent decades to become the most innovative building material; seek advice on non- or reflective glass, or glass that allows those inside to see out but is opaque to anyone looking in. It is photosensitive, darkening as light intensifies and lightening when light levels are low. Glass today can interact with climate and make optimum use of energy. Damien Hirst used LCD (Liquid Crystal Display) glass in his studio which turns opaque on entry. Azman Owens architects used this system for the changing rooms in Alexander McQueen's fashion store on London's Conduit Street.

Windows are part of the infrastructure of a home and cannot be considered alone. Most of us start with window treatments, unless building from scratch or on a very high budget. Dressing down is the way forward. As planning strictures on earlier buildings preserve facades (resulting in diversity of window shapes), windows are often a given, but they can be modernised by interior treatment. Blinds, shutters, scrim, there are many ways to keep harsh light out and heat in. Windows themselves can be costly but treatments need not be.

***This page, top*** These windows are not quite what they seem: on the right is a real window, but the other is a cupboard door. The large window on the far left, with its integrated circular mirror, views the kitchen.

***This page, bottom*** The British throw windows outward and have curtains; the French open them inward and use shutters, which allow ventilation but keep sunlight out. A smart choice for character is plantation shutters. These make a change from blinds, and suit a lofty room.

***Opposite, top left*** In this restored English barn the bathroom enjoys a window wall on to a tiny courtyard. Plain glass is better in bathrooms than textured glass that is hard to clean.

***Opposite, top right*** The thick straw-bale walls of this award-winning barn conversion, plaster-coated inside, are pierced with small windows at shoulder height on the shady side of the barn. On the sunny side is a wall of windows.

***Opposite, bottom left*** A rough-cut square in a wall is highly effective in this up-to-the-minute room in an ancient building. Glass pantiles (curved roofing tiles) throughout the building add light.

***Opposite, bottom right*** Round porthole-like windows belonged with Modernist and Art Deco architecture but are seeing a revival. This hinge is to one side, but portholes can tilt into their frame, which makes for good balance.

***Above*** Post-and-beam architecture comprises wooden (or steel) poles, sheet glass and louvred-glass panels for air circulation, allowing glorious play of light throughout a building. This Californian example dates from the early 1960s; building such houses is now prohibited in the state.

***Above right*** Internal windows can be misused in conversions, but here is a successful interior window in a small loftlike space: the bed quarters are above, the bathroom underneath, and the living space visible from both. As well as bringing light, internal windows add a sense of space and accessibility.

***Right*** In this renovated 1860s townhouse, all work was permitted by Landmark law except removal of front-of-house windows. Shutters, especially the hinged variety whose flaps fold completely on one another, suit sash windows. Window treatments are often constrained by radiators or air-conditioning units.

***Opposite*** Also in California, Mark Rios's floor-to-ceiling windows echo mid-century Modernist experiments with curtain walls (walls made up almost entirely of windows rather than masonry) and picture windows (where a window takes up a significant portion of a wall, generally with a magnificent view).

***Above*** An L-shaped barn in Norfolk in England has been turned into two separate living units. There is no point in attempting to conceal that this is a barn; even if an up-to-date interior is desired, it is preferable to make use of exposed beams, which in fact here complement the modern elements while retaining a sense of place.

***Above*** For weight reduction, metal beams are formed as an "I" shape, with a thin vertical web and thicker horizontal flanges where the metal is most useful. They were called I beams, but modern flanges are wider so they are now often called wide-flange beams. As a vertical support, this is perhaps more characterful than the classic I beam.

***Above*** The appearance of heavy-duty metal or wood or a combination, as here, gives solidity to an industrial space and reminds us of its former use. Both metal and wooden surfaces complement smooth concrete and poured floors, but can also be a welcome contrast to softer finishes. Polished steel looks flimsy and more rarefied in comparison.

***Above*** Architect Anthony Hudson has built walkways to the upper level of a nineteenth-century former barn. This bridge spans the living room and connects bedrooms and bathrooms, allowing a dramatic double-height ceiling for the living and dining space. The device appears suspended in midair, the railings and bars the same on each side.

# elements

Structural elements are necessary, and are not always "evils"; it is up to us how they look. There are arguments for keeping within the existing structure if you can, one being that, in general, services remain intact, another being the aesthetic coherence. Whether original or added, steel supports, wooden beams and concrete columns are all structural elements but bring texture to a room. The exposure of their tactile nature, because of their form and surface, means they can make the room appear very different. A steel support can give an industrial edge, a perfect tubular column a hint of the *piloti*s used in Modern architecture, a wooden beam a nod to more ancient history. So these elements must be considered as surfaces within room design, not just as practical supports.

***Above*** Some pillars not only support ceilings but conceal pipes or cables. Whatever their reason for being, they can be spruced up, made more elegant, with plaster, stainless steel or other surfaces. Designer Marina Frisenna, in a rural house for a large family near Liège in Belgium, has used them as contemporary embellishment.

***Above*** Pilasters (rectangular vertical supports by a wall, with base and capital), piers (vertical supports, more massive than columns) and pillars (more slender) are all non-circular. Columns, slender freestanding or self-supporting elements, can be circular. They may be stone, steel, concrete or brick; in wood, a column is a post and rarely supports.

***Above*** A beam is just a beam, or is it? In structural engineering, a beam is a horizontal member that spans an opening and carries a loading. If this loading is a brick or a stone wall, the beam is called a lintel or lintel beam. If it carries a floor or a roof load, the beam is a floor joist or roof joist. Beams can meet to share loads in many ways.

***Above*** At one end of a large living room in a London townhouse, architect Michael Wolfson compartmentalised the music area (complete with grand piano as star attraction) by creating a box within the space. Its non-structural walls and ceiling are also home to attractive niches that act as bases for ornamentation.

If you are dealing with an industrial space, beams and supports are generally going to have to be lived with, although they can be boxed in. There are choices for all kinds of homes but some come at a price. The trick is to emphasise good features and minimise or remove the worst. Identify the positive aspects of a feature, then decide upon remedial action: is it to be a minor procedure or a major operation? For instance, if you remove a wall or supporting column, the area must then be spanned with a supporting horizontal beam, columns, piers, pillars or other supports; these will probably be more successful visually if incorporated into your interior plan rather than semi-concealed. Do bear in mind whether what you are doing is legal. Then make the most of the structural elements that can add to surface texture and delineate space.

# services

In the modern world we tend to take services – water, heat and light – for granted, and only of late have we seriously considered the consequences of a world where resources are depleting and how to create new and better sources of energy. We are wiser to the problems the use of nuclear energy might bring, and seek alternatives in hydroelectric power, geothermic generation and newer techniques in wave-powered electrical generation, for example. Some seek solutions in solar and wind power (solar power is becoming cheaper; the silicone wafers it uses have been pricey). And we are taking more responsibility for our planet, whether it is in the simple gathering of kitchen spoils for the recycling bin, or in better understanding how to insulate the home so energy is not carelessly dissipated. Sometimes it might be wise to take *New Scientist* magazine to bed when thinking about building a home in order to be better informed, rather than a stylish journal that merely advertises rich pickings and visual inspiration of various kinds on the home-decoration front.

My husband and I have recently been trying to find a weekend home in Brittany, which offers delightful nature: the colours – the greens, greys and blues – of this northern French region are particularly inviting, and the coarseness of the Atlantic Ocean appeals enormously after the relatively pathetic moans of the English Channel and Mediterranean. We have decided that, aside from location – which has a lot to do with the exact positioning of the building, and thus the natural light it offers – we have just two other immediate prerequisites: electricity and water (and with water we include waste disposal). Numerous properties exist without these vital elements installed, but we have decided that although we will retile roofs, lay slate or stone on what are often still earth floors, and build walls, supports and staircases (with professional help), we are not prepared to take on absolutely raw space without electricity and water. To rewire is fine, of course, and essential, but the service must be there. Some people do take on raw space, but because as a couple we like to be quite hands-on when building or renovating (my husband, who was brought up in New Zealand, where there is still plenty of land, has built six houses from scratch – I have been more of a renovator and restorer through provenance – although we do plan, eventually, to build our ultimate modern home) and we like to be there to make on-the-spot decisions, those two home comforts will make all the difference to how much time we initially spend at the house, when the building work is happening, and how soon the property will be complete.

Water, heat and light are essential to living, and only the very brave should attempt even a short period of time without close access to these facilities. This said, we did, when staying with a friend recently in France, have a power cut that left us illuminated by candles, warmed by the fire and fed by the barbecue – and the saving grace was the superior cladding around the hot-water system, which retained heat in the water for five days. Conclusion: man cannot live on food and water alone; we need good cladding too.

# water

Showering has taken over from bathing as a morning activity since it is invigorating and takes less time and water. Trickling showers are no longer acceptable: power pumps provide pressure and aerate water for what commercials describe as a "champagne effect". The market is dominated by electric, mixer and power showers. Electric ones are less expensive and less impressive, but give an instantaneous shower, drawing water from a cold mains supply and heating only the water used (thus ideal for homes without stored hot water). Mixer showers (including bath/shower mixers) draw hot and cold water from the household supply, and suit homes with a ready supply of hot water or a combination boiler or multipoint water heater, if water pressure is strong enough. Shower pumps can boost performance on any good-quality mixer shower. A power shower takes water from both hot and cold sources and pumps it out at greater pressure, so suits homes with a cold storage tank and a ready supply of hot water. For both power and mixer showers, water supplies must be gravity-fed from a storage tank of at least 112 litres (25 gallons).

NewTeam (a subsidiary of Masco Corporation USA) champions its Venturi shower, which passes cold mains water through a jet pump with such high velocity and pressure that it sucks in hot water from the household cylinder. This is ideal for houses with low water pressure.

An elegant choice is the shower dome, a large fixed "rose" on the ceiling or at least well above head height. In Claridge's hotel in London, the domes are enormous and a second dome pummels you from the wall at waist height: utterly refreshing.

# baths

Bathing has become an evening washing activity, since baths offer relaxation (most bath products confirm this: there are more of the aromatherapeutic variety to put us to sleep than to invigorate on the market, although aromatherapy claims to do both). For added comfort there are rules of thumb regarding how much space is required for bathing activity aside from basins and baths: this is said to be, for an adult, approximately 100 x 70 centimetres (40 x 28 inches) for drying oneself in front of the bath or basin, and 80 x 65 centimetres (32 x 26 inches) in front of a lavatory or bidet.

Baths themselves are now rarely the standard size (167 centimetres/66 inches long) they used to be in the West (in Japan, the deep hot tubs have a footprint no larger than a conventional shower: one sits in a tub rather than lying). Since designers and architects have been increasing bathroom size of late, larger and more unusual baths can be accommodated. Some opt for a short, deep bath (almost Japanese style), often freestanding with water supplies from the floor, as far as practicable, or giving the illusion at least, which usually means attached to only one wall on the narrow length.

***Previous page*** Glass is good for a modern basin where other materials are earthy (the background is Indian slate). Usually standard greenish glass, called plain float glass, as here, is used; what appears to be clear glass, which is low-iron glass, is a special order. A similar effect can be achieved using Lucite.

***Far left*** French supplier Volevatch provided materials for this London bathroom: Stone, St Martin "Patiné", was used throughout. The bath is a roll-top, although inserted into the surround.

***Left*** The oldest bathtub allegedly pertains to the palace of Knossos in Crete, from 1700 BC. Its similarity to modern tubs is astounding, as is its plumbing. Today's traditional tubs are made from materials such as porcelain or enamel.

***Left, below*** A pull-out shower is the neat solution in a small bathroom, as here in Paris. These days stylised mixer taps are common, some with a revolving faucet. Accessories define the style of a bathroom and add the finishing touch.

***This page*** The custom-designed freestanding deep red resin bath in architect Fred Collin's London home is quite a statement. He found it at the 100% Design fair in London: it had to be shipped from Helsinki and took six weeks and a crane to lift it.

***This page*** In New York, this one-piece purpose-built Corian basin has faucets and (not seen here) shower fittings by Arne Jacobson. The rest of the room comprises high-gloss white formica doors to conceal ash timber-lined cabinetry and steel doors to the garden.

***Opposite, top*** A very different New York bathroom with an apparently rough-hewn stone basin. Limestone works well in a bathroom or wet room (the fashionable term for an entirely waterproof room, with floor and sometimes basins sloping).

***Opposite, bottom left*** A sculptural cube basin surround in square tiles, in a bathroom by Laurent Buttazzoni in Paris. Visible from the guest bedroom, it had to be attractive. Planning regulations on separation of bathrooms from other areas vary from country to country.

***Opposite, bottom right*** The sliding mirrored door from a bedroom opens to reveal an adjoining bathroom in this Manhattan apartment by architect Bruce Bierman. A bathroom with two basins allows the luxury of washing and dressing together.

# basins

From visiting new homes the world over, I conclude that "his 'n' hers" is back with a vengeance: this time not monogrammed slippers or towelling robes but twin or double basins. A pair of troughs side by side seems less popular than an elongated trough sporting two sets of taps, but is seen quite regularly, although twin basins do require more wall space. I imagine the popularity of such basins is not because we are skimping on bathroom space – bathrooms are getting bigger (until Edwardian times at least, in grander homes a couple would keep separate bathrooms and dressing rooms, sometimes even bedrooms) – but because we share time differently, appreciating all time spent with a loved one, even time spent on ablution.

With dual-income lives (some of us have children too) perhaps the bathroom is the new social venue for a couple to squeeze extra time together. The bathroom chat in the twenty-first century is taking the place of the martini at six. A friend of mine says the only time her husband is static when awake, hence their only conversation time, is when he is showering.

***Above left*** Double basins can be nicely streamlined, and accommodate more bathroom utensils and paraphernalia than a regular sink. I like both the twin and the double basin and twin or double mirror, but I think the surrounds should be left uncluttered. A simple basin is always best, its form depending upon material, and must be shallow enough from wall to front to allow use of the mirror.

***Left*** A large stone bathroom basin is set on a dark wood countertop in this master bathroom in Milan. Both pieces are by Boffi, as are all the bathroom fixtures. Pipes are concealed by stone. The wooden floor, treated with waterproof varnish to give a pale milky finish, has a marble border. Areas under sinks should be uncluttered.

***Above*** This hand-washing facility is neat in a small bathroom. Bathroom suppliers provide only basic installation, so the best idea is to select fittings from builder's suppliers, then piece together accessories that complete the look. It can be a challenge to find compatibile hardware and fixtures, particularly if ordering items from different countries.

***Right*** The principal bathroom in this Paris pied-à-terre is at one end of the apartment, and leads from the living room, so has to be smart for guests. A walk-around basin, set in Carrara marble, takes the system away from the walls.

***This page*** An unusual circular stainless-steel double sink in a Paris kitchen. A double sink separates food from cleaning. SieMatic produces twin-bowl stainless circular sinks; Franke has similar but more square designs. Both SieMatic and Franke produce small-scale apparatus, and both, unlike most manufacturers, combine taps and bowls, creating a more integrated product. SieMatic takes inspiration from the Bauhaus.

***Right*** Large rectangular sinks are often used for soaking fish or vegetables. These, designed by architect Vincent Van Duysen, are recessed into white Carrara marble which has been given a matte polish, with a chrome tap by Vola. Marble and stone are popular but expensive choices. Corian can be an alternative: it combines natural minerals with acrylic to produce worktop surfaces that are made to fit seamlessly around sinks.

***Right, below*** When designing a kitchen, you have to think about water, gas and electrical circuitry. Here the problem of kitchen and bathroom plumbing is solved in one: the kitchen sinks are directly through the wall from the bathroom basin, which is situated on the other side of this window with its circular mirror.

# sinks

Until very recently, the kitchen was the most rudimentary of rooms the world over, used for heating food but not cleaning it. The ancient Greeks and Romans introduced boiling and stewing, with water from bottles or vessels, but kitchen sinks are new indeed.

The first considerations when choosing a sink, if it is not part of an overall system by a firm such as Boffi, Tsunami or Bulthaup (the Germans seem to have a monopoly on good kitchen design), are the amount of space, the number of basins required and the type of material that will suit the overall design. Today most sinks are made of stainless steel (the styles offered by Franke are super), but stoneware and synthetic materials are also employed.

Some designs provide a large sink and a smaller one; others have a built-in colander or a tray that forms another work surface (which adds to a small kitchen but confuses a larger one – two sinks are always better). Sinks and counters in a solid piece optimise cleanliness. Tap choices are numerous: apart from traditional dual taps, there are long-stem versions, mixers and rotators. Long-stem taps are practical, pull-out ones highly useful.

A new concept is Rieber's "water station", a floor-to-waist cylindrical unit with up to four sinks. It requires a large kitchen, but this is the future. With today's well-designed accessories, there is no excuse not to be streamlined.

# heat

Fire's extraordinary usefulness and equally extraordinary dangers impress every human being from infancy onwards. Ordinary fire is the rapid chemical combination of oxygen with carbon and other substances in such a way that heat, flame and light are produced. In a broader sense fire is the "process" whereby the combination of one chemical element with another, when reduced to a gaseous mass, produces heat and flame: it forms the basis of most forms of modern manufacturing and transportation (older versions too – have you seen the images of men stoking the massive fires on the *Titanic*?) and has been a powerful agent in determining the spread and present distribution of mankind.

Curiously, there are still tribes who suffer serious loss if their fires are extinguished: among certain inhabitants of Papua New Guinea who have no means of kindling a blaze, live coals of slow-burning wood are preserved in their huts. If these go out, the coastal dwellers must go to the mountains to find people who understand how to make fire. They then return with burning coals. Australian aborigines prefer to make long journeys to another tribe to find fire rather than undertake the laborious (as they see it) making of it themselves.

In the modern world, we have high expectations in terms of temperature, and do not function well if we are either too cold or too hot. Well-insulated surfaces are important here since they reflect back low-temperature heat. But we also rely on a sophisticated range of heating apparatuses that extend far beyond the simple power and charm of fire.

# fire

According to Greek legend, Prometheus brought fire to Earth, having lit a torch from the Sun's chariot. On the Cook Islands near New Zealand, the Polynesian Maui is said to have obtained fire by visiting Hell, where he learned to rub sticks together. In many cultures, the bringer of fire is seen as a hero: periodic loss of fire is part of the ceremony found in the Catholic and Greek Orthodox churches (church lights are all extinguished during Passion Week and then "new fire" is made, from which all fires for the following year must be made). The loss of fire has always been regarded as a tragedy.

"It is certain that no fireless tribe of men has been found.... Man is scarcely man until he is in possession of fire," suggested W.G. Sumner and A.G. Keller in their 1927 article "The Science of Society". But how in possession of fire? We cherished fire long before learning to create it, making use of fires engendered by falling meteors, lightning, volcanic eruptions and the friction of avalanches. We soon realised the value of fire for warding off animals, cooking food and keeping warm.

***Previous page*** With real fires the air for combustion is an important consideration in fireplace design. A throat restrictor and tray can mean an under-hearth draught that draws air from outside, not from the room. Gas fires are the smart alternative now, clean and efficient.

***Below*** This marble fireplace, original to the 1860s Manhattan townhouse, retains its sobriety and solidity but also adds a focal point. Thankfully, new fireplaces today are not stuck in a time warp, but if you have a decent fireplace, why not utilise it?

***Right*** Christian and Carolyn Van Outersterp, husband-and-wife team behind CVO Fireplaces, have installed their own design into a Victorian surround in their home in Newcastle, in the north of England.

***Far right*** Wood-burning stoves exist in many guises and there are gas-fired equivalents (Thermocet's run on natural or propane gas; Piazzetta makes highly contemporary versions). The surface area maximises heat convection. This log-burning stove, made by Norfolk Stoves in England, is quaint and efficient.

***Opposite, top left*** In the unusual home of CVO Fireplaces' founders is the "Ripple" fireplace. It is cast in concrete with a Portland stone finish, 2 metres (7 feet) high. The roller-blind fireguard is stainless steel.

***Opposite, top right*** CVO's fireplaces come in many materials: lead-crystal glass, cast iron, bronze and concrete. For this one, for a kitchen, a thick slab of green Rio Verde slate from Brazil at waist height forms a barbecue. Its concave centre is hand carved.

***Opposite, bottom left*** This bedroom fireplace, "Slit and Slab" from CVO, almost passes as collage. The tiny dancing flames, on micro-fibre developed by space-shuttle engineers, are so hologramlike that glass was added to protect the unwary.

***Opposite, bottom right*** Contemporary country chic, this floor of pebbles in resin houses underfloor heating. A wood-burning stove gives added heat. The building benefits from insulating panels faced with clear glass-fibre sheeting.

***This page, top left*** This fireplace in Brussels by Van Duysen is a simple floor-level recess. Gas-fired, its temperature is adjusted by remote control. The Platonic Fireplace Company produces designs like this.

***This page, top right*** With repopularisation of the fireplace (central heating had led to its neglect), fire grills, fire-dogs, irons and tongs have also reappeared. Traditional can work, if less fussy than the surround.

***This page, bottom*** The CVO "Firebowl" is an iconic piece, winner of a Prince of Wales Medal and exhibited at RIBA and the Victoria and Albert Museum. Available in various shapes and materials (here concrete), it can run on wood, coal or gas: this one is gas-fired.

# radiators

People are happiest when their feet are warmer than, or at least as warm as, their heads. Insulate floors first, then install systems that either heat the floor or have an output near the ground. Convected and radiated heat are different: a combination of the two works well in a temperate climate. Heating that combines both may be a radiator or heated floors and ceilings; a radiant heater (electric, gas, oil or coal fire) should be installed for severe chills.

The surface area of radiators must relate to the volume of the room. The outputs of different species of radiators varies, but one large single radiator will provide considerably less warmth than skirting radiators of exactly the same capacity spread evenly around a room. Every part of the room should be comfortable to use, so eliminate draughts and insulate windows as much as possible, although ventilation is also important.

If you select a warm-air heating system you will need to install a humidifier, since dry air irritates skin and eyes, can damage furniture and artefacts, and causes shrinkage in wood panelling. Low-temperature heat sources cause less damage than high-temperature ones – another reason to spread the heat.

***Opposite, top left*** Nothing is quite as glamorous as a radiator when you look at the selections offered by Aestus, whose sculptural forms (look out for the "Demitour Papillon" which looks like a bow tie) suit any space, or Caradon Stelrad (whose "Optia" towel rail is a shelf unit too), or the more appropriately named Myson towel warmers.

***Opposite, bottom left*** The humble towel rail is indispensable. This is a simplified "ladder" system (you can find multiple-rung and curved varieties). Most firms offer at least six sizes. It is good to go for the option of an electric heating element so the towel rail can be warm even when the heating is off.

***Opposite, bottom right*** This "wet room" is a delight: ostensibly a shower in a room which leads to the garden through double doors. Greenery is abundant. The vanity unit appears supported by the chrome radiator beneath the countertop, freeing up wall space, which either may not be there or need not be hindered.

***This page*** In a scheme by Marina Frisenna in Belgium, radiators are very much part of the wall art, some, like this, many metres high (it is two-thirds the height of the lofty ground floor), the space it heats vast. There was a fad for incorporating radiators into recesses or built into shelving, which is neither pleasant nor effective. Thermostatic controls on radiators make heat output adjustable, and, in larger houses, radiator circuits for each floor are separated so the controls operate independently.

# light

We cannot physically live without heat or water, and fire brings light (and a focal point) too. Goodness knows man existed with candle and gaslight before Thomas Edison was accredited with his light bulb. But as sophisticates, we have now studied the effect light can have on man: we understand the effect of SAD or Seasonal Affective Disorder on the mind (it is caused by a biochemical imbalance in the hypothalamus due to the lack of sunshine in winter), how the lack of sunlight or an equivalent can make us miserable. We know that man is phototropic and walks towards light, and science has taught us that light can mould our sighted lives and alter our spatial awareness in so many ways.

Much of our information about the external world is gained through the visual sense, and therefore adequate lighting is of major importance in everyday life. We must concern ourselves with the way the eye responds to stimulation by light, and it is good to do the homework about this very complicated field. When designing your home, consider that the amount of detail in a scene that can be perceived by the eye is closely related to the illumination. For example, in order to read small print, a high level of illumination is required. Light theory is a minefield, which is why we have specialists to help us. Lighting systems, to be effective, should be designed by a professional. The home owner's job is to select the lamps and hardware once the scheme has been designed. When selecting other objects for the home, do also bear in mind that colours appear very different in different kinds of light.

***Previous page*** Brooklyn-based David Weeks's lighting products include floor lamps and elaborate chandeliers and sconces reminiscent of the lights of Serge Mouille. Part decorative and sculptural, his multi-armed light illuminates in different and alterable directions, the pod shells acting as up- and downlighting.

***Right*** Handblown Murano-glass lights by architect Michele de Lucchi for Produzione Privata. Available in sandblasted and silver versions, green and milk glass too, the "Acquatinta" suspension light in clear glass is often applied in multiples.

***Opposite, top left*** In a kitchen, a swivelling downlighter sends a beam on to a worksurface. The appropriate amount of light for an activity is affected by the angle of light, its colour and the spatial distribution in both immediate environment and distant view.

***Opposite, top right*** Uplighters bring diffuse reflected light to a room and give an illusion of space. They may be floor-, table- or wall-mounted, and are good for stairwells or corridors. Their luminous intensity distribution is often asymmetric (a must if wall-mounted), and they are not suitable for ceilings lower than 2.5 metres (8 feet) unless careful attention is paid to avoid uneven light intensity.

***Opposite, bottom*** Poul Henningsen based his design on analysis of lampshade function: the size, shape and position of the shades determine light and glare. His "Louvre", "Kugle" and "Artichoke" lamps are available in re-edition from Louis Poulsen; originals, as here, are highly collectible.

# Lights

What is the difference between a lamp and a light? For me the former is an object that can be shifted while the latter is attached, part of a "structural" lighting scheme. A lamp can add ambient lighting; lights are more hard-working (with the exception of desk lamps dedicated to task lighting).

Light orchestrates our perception of form, colour and texture. Brightness is about contrasts, and in establishing these it is vital to observe the effect of light on materials (wall and floor finishes first, others later). An ill-lit room will appear distorted; good lighting can reapportion space and lead us from room to room.

"Furniture, style, carpets, everything in the home is unimportant compared to the positioning of the lighting. It doesn't cost money to light a room correctly, but it does require culture," said Danish designer Poul Henningsen (1894–1967). The first lighting expert of the twentieth century, he encapsulated lighting theory in his 1924 "PH" lamp, a multi-shade lamp assembled so that shades covered the bulb yet rays emerged without being reflected more than once. In the form of either a ceiling-hung light or a table lamp or standard lamp (the inside painted red to soften the light), it also gave general lighting, so the contrast between room and, for instance, table was not too harsh. Henningsen had to introduce his lamps in public buildings and offices before they were accepted for the home.

***Opposite, top left*** This extraordinary double-globe basketweave shade is a low-tech solution that adds gentle ambient illumination. It is produced for Assiatide and made in Thailand.

***Opposite, top right*** The drama of this dressing room comes from shocking blue fluorescent strips. Much wasted energy in office buildings is due to poor fluorescent-lighting fixtures that scatter up to 85 percent of the light.

***This page, top left*** These ceiling spots are from Modular Lighting in Belgium. By night, the ceiling seems to recede; by day, the cables stitch the space together, an art form in themselves.

***This page, top right*** The human eye can cope with a wide range of brightness but not all at once. These spotlights are effective day and night, the contrast level controlled by a dimmer.

***Opposite, bottom left*** Soft ambient light emanates from two ceiling-to-floor box columns. Pairs of lamps usually denote a passageway. This pair actively anchors the room.

***Opposite, bottom right*** The first striking use of fluorescent tubes was in Bauhaus lamps. Here a pair of tubes brings up-tempo sentiment to a bathroom. I am reminded of a visit to India, where I was aghast at fluorescent tubes loosely strung up in roadside trees.

***This page, bottom left*** Downlighters, generally 10–20 percent more efficient than uplighting, provide strong beams of light for a stairwell.

***This page, bottom right*** Do not underestimate the generosity of natural light. English architect Sir John Soane (1753–1837) controlled its quality via coloured-glass skylights and domes to warm the grey northern light.

# lamps

At the beginning of an interior project we think, "lights, action, music", but rarely "lamp" – that comes towards the end when we finally collapse on to our re-edition Eileen Gray sofa with a rather stiff drink. There is an exception to every rule, and although lights are fitted and lamps are not, I do consider the odd decorative wall sconce as a lamp, particularly if it is there more for its own pleasure, sitting pretty, than for us to see by. But, in general, lamps are found on tables or in cosy corners, to help successful grouping of furniture and thus people. I do not see the point to putting them on mantelpieces, since ambient lumination should come from the fire after dark (and during the day, a room should be adequately lit by daylight).

In principle, there are two ways to light a room: by uniform illumination, which roughly mimics the effect daylight would have, or by placing lights according to convenience and artfulness. The first philosophy can be impressive, and sometimes intrusive. A more imaginative result comes, I believe, by using artificial light in different ways throughout a home, perhaps using a combination of lights and lamps, as described in the second philosophy. Furthermore, I tend to agree with Poul Henningsen, who did not "subscribe to the idea of an ever-increasing demand for more powerful lighting intensity".

***Opposite, top left*** Frédéric Méchiche brings severe geometry to this room with a "framed" lamp. It has become quite a pastime for the French to add cube or box-form lights and lamps.

***Opposite, top right*** This pretty string of lights revels in its connections. The inventor of the first light bulb was Heinrich Goebal, a clockmaker from Hanover who emigrated to New York. In 1854, he made a charred bamboo fibre glow in a vacuum-sealed perfume bottle. As there was no electricity network, he could only light his own shop window.

***Opposite, bottom*** Frenchman Jacques Adnet was known for top-stitched, leather-covered pieces: not only lamps but also tables, desks and coat hooks, created in the 1940s and 1950s for Hermès. These are rare and significant early "lifestyle" collections.

***Above*** Sculptural lamps grace Ralph Pucci's upstate New York house. His firm represents lamp designers Chris Lehrecke (slimline wood), Christophe Delcourt (severe metal), John Wigmore (architectural lighting) and David Weeks (fluid metal).

***Above right*** A classic moves with time, so do not be afraid to mingle old and new. Old lamps can be spruced up with an elegant shade: sheer and black is always good, as long as the shade is wide enough to allow light out.

***Right*** These unusual sconces are parchment, from the skin of sheep or goats (the term can also mean paper). Vellum (more delicate skin), parchment and paper are all effective diffusing materials for light.

***This page*** A vintage industrial wall-mounted task lamp in polished nickel finish can swing to illuminate either the bedside desk or a reader in bed. Many vintage stores have a wide selection of task lamps; this one is from Wyeth in New York's SoHo.

***Opposite, top left*** A cross between reading lamp, torch and sconce, a pair of tiny lights perch above the bed, the vision more boutique hotel than home. In a Victorian interior, even if bereft of latterday embellishment, it is easy to add a touch of modernity with small lamps.

***Opposite, top right*** Traditional-looking, counter-balanced, anglepoise or other office lamps can be found at markets. The original "Anglepoise" (based on human limbs, with a spring as muscles) was made by Herbert Terry in 1933 and designed by automotive engineer George Carwardine. These two are office lamps but not anglepoise.

***Opposite, bottom left*** The "Duplex" lamp, in brushed stainless steel with a paper lampshade, was designed for Ecart International by Andrée Putman. A smart freestanding lamp used for ambient lighting, it is extremely stable, a welcome addition to this seating arrangement in a New York scheme by Bruce Bierman Design. The Ecart range is stocked by Pucci International in New York.

***Opposite, bottom right*** Artemide's classic "Tolomeo" is the architect's choice: it is lightweight and can be formed into various angles. This is a floor-standing version; some clip to desks, others are table-standing or even wall spots. The "Tolomeo" was designed in 1987 by Michele de Lucchi and Giancarlo Fassina.

FORSYTH
CRAIS

# storage

Two American women, Emily Dickinson (1830–6) and Gertrude Stein (1874–1946), were innovative precursors of modernist poetry and prose, yet to this day canonical criticism avoids both their names and work. Dickinson, a recluse, worked without interest from peers. Her poems were almost all unpublished in her lifetime and only discovered in boxes after her death. She felt, as she confessed in a poem in 1862, "they shut me up in prose – As when a little girl They put me in the closet – Because they liked me 'still'."

Stein, by contrast, was an influential patron of the arts, thrived on company and enjoyed her literary celebrity; influenced by Cézanne, Picasso and Cubism, she elaborated on visual invention verbally, her poetry an open collage expressing life and living.

Both women questioned who should police grammar and shut us inside the structure of a sentence. But where Dickinson experienced many kinds of confinement, Stein possibly knew only the general confinement of women of her time. Better to be moving than still, I say. Better, too, not to store evidence of a talent in boxes.

The most movable parts of a home are objects that require storage. Our home reflects our lives, habits and souls – and how fortunate we are today to be able to punctuate as we see fit, without fear of moralistic criticism. There should be no right way to create one's space, one's life, only expression.

Closets conceal our elements for living, and some of us have more baggage along than others. In my parents' home, my mother exposes hers on tabletops: inkwell collections in myriad coloured glass, miniature boxes, her home is crushed with antiques and swathed in fabric. My home is simpler, the storage space the only place where multiples of anything can be seen: freshly laundered towels (dark green), crisp Egyptian-cotton sheets with faggoting for edges (white), glasses (uniform) and white china plates with gold trim, mismatched on purpose. Neither statement is right or wrong; it is not only what you store but how you store it that makes for elegant living.

In our house, the television is behind doors, toys in the boys' room, for the main part in the closet (their bedroom is open-plan, occupying the top floor), and we have paperless offices in the basement. I look forward to a wireless house, but in the mean time, even our cables and wires are "plumbed in".

The first step to successful storage is to prune your possessions. New habits learned will prevent you from piling clutter in the future. Bathroom storage is simpler to organise than in other rooms; the kitchen is a minefield of multiple activities. Books, by the way, should never be behind glass (confined, they cannot breathe) and should always be within reach. Keeping belongings ordered has become a spiritual quest – no longer a dull necessity, storage is a creative pursuit. Space is precious and technology abundant: we have to accommodate functional gadgetry. Where storage used to mean "confining" an object until required, we now have to "store" equipment (television, computer, music system) that lives on in its encasement. No-one removes a television from its storage space: it is adapted for use within it. Good storage solutions are key to a smooth-running home and a stress-free existence.

***Opposite*** In private investor Martin Harding's home, this custom-made wall-recessed cabinet, in maple wood with cherry inlay, contains a huge television (centre panel), DVD, DHS, video satellite equipment, controls for indoor and outdoor music, and sofa blankets.

***Left*** A highly contemporary solution in a London dining room: a cantilevered storage unit/shelf. Its ends are glass, and are illuminated by night. This streamlining adds to the room.

***Above left*** Solutions are also necessary for storage of a single unit. Here, an attractive box opens to reveal a television that swings out on a turntable for viewing from different angles in a small space.

***Above*** A built-in cabinet spans a wall but does not have to be recessed into it. If you do not require an entire wall expanse of concealed storage, you may want to utilise the space for open storage of ornaments and books.

# leisure

Storage meets display in the living room, the one room you might wish to ornament above others. How do you store all the accoutrements related to both entertaining and relaxing without overpowering a space that depends on its handsome looks? The configuration of your home dictates the kind of storage you need: if you have a library, it is unlikely you will need bookshelves in the drawing room, while open-plan living might require that a room accommodates sideboard, telephone table and mini-bar all-in-one unit. Make sure your storage happily coexists with the decoration and architectural style of your home without compromising the visual impact of any room or its function of relaxation. Three words are useful when working out how much storage to incorporate into a scheme: balance, scale and perspective.

Although blanket boxes, trunks and lidded baskets are assumed movable, they tend not to be once filled. They also manage to clutter the floor space. The best way forward is to create vertical storage without upsetting the overall footprint of the room. Occasionally it can be useful to incorporate a piece of furniture into the room which has an added storage element, say a drawer

beneath a coffee table so a magazine or newspaper can be stashed away at a moment's notice (do remember to remove it later). But on the whole, go for modular living, where the storage plan is part of the fibre of the home. Built-in units are customised to your requirements and can be expensive – and should be so if they are built to last in the manner of the great craftsmen – although some freestanding furniture can be added which actually enhances the space. Furniture can carve up space very nicely, and a bookcase perpendicular to a wall can easily conceal a home office.

Build cupboards and drawers once you know what you are enclosing: a television or sound system must fit snugly so no space is wasted, but hi-fi units emit heat and need to breathe. Cabinets that do not allow air to circulate need perforations. Bear in mind that manufacturer's specifications may not include wiring, which may take up significant space: if in doubt, check exact requirements with an electrician. Storage-unit doors may also require additional clearance to open, depending on the type of door and the way it slides, swings or rolls, so measure accurately and plan carefully.

***Above*** An office-cum-workroom space answers the needs of a couple passionate about creative reference books. The more formal living and media rooms house their glass and movie collections.

***Right*** Shelves in coves or niches do not inhibit floor space and can be put to many uses. There is a vogue for shelves of a single size, to create an architectural effect. But different-height shelves can look less gappy with different-height books.

***Opposite*** Shelves with dividers keep books upright and breakables secure. In earthquake, airport or rail zones, large pieces are best secured with straps, smaller pieces with "earthquake putty", or museum wax, available in clear gel for glass shelves. Rubber shelf liners can also prevent slip.

Arts d'Afrique

***Top left*** Some units, such as this wall-to-wall closet in Paris, contain more than just clothes. The evidence of clothes is the carpet, for dressing in comfort. The custom-designed unit floats above the floor and below the ceiling, its texture adding to its artistry.

***Top centre*** Sliding doors save space in a narrow room. A his 'n' hers dressing room works best if clothes are separated to each side, as here. Try to arrange them so as to minimise closing and reopening doors.

***Top right*** A 1930s-inspired curved wall has been created for clothes in a Victorian city house. Curtains are inexpensive, and work well here, but makeshift, lightweight structures are a poor substitute for a closet, visually and structurally.

***Bottom left*** This closet is strikingly simple, almost pretty. It was banged together quickly but effectively, its front just four painted planks of timber. Beware antique closets that are not deep enough for shoulders of today.

***Bottom centre*** If you have the space, this closet is the ultimate storage facility, allowing quick and easy selection. With clothes this neat, there is not always need for a closet door.

***Bottom right*** Here, classic wall-to-wall closets take up an entire wall. Within are various heights of unit and drawers. Folded sweaters take less space than hung ones, so ensure you have adequate box-shaped units.

# clothing

Today we have far more specialised clothes than any generation before us; utility, workwear, casual and sport. We also wear different lengths so need different-length hangings. Having come from a background of store design, I am constantly aware of how adaptable a closet must be. Most of us have to deal with seasonal change too, and the question of whether to change the entire closet over to a new season, and if so, when? The ideal is to keep a pristine dressing room or walk-in closet with everything on view, a partly mirrored inner sanctum from which you emerge groomed to the hilt. The reality is that most of us have to contain clothing in a bedroom, hallway or bathroom. Since these rooms may be on upper levels, in houses at least, carving out storage from eaves, corners and walls can be a good opportunity to rethink how best to utilise space. Caring for clothes helps make them last.

Work your closet space so accessories for your head are at head height, and place shirts and jackets above counterpart bottom halves. Shoes are usually best on tall, sturdy shelving units, like bookshelves. Place ties and belts on one side, also vertically and roughly at waist height to avoid bending down. You should be able to access your clothes with very little movement.

***This page*** In a design by Bruce Bierman Inc, all kitchen facilities bar the countertop hob are on a single wall. The refrigerator is concealed behind the door to the right of the sink, the only give-away the vent beneath; even washed dishes are concealed. Doors open to a push touch.

***Opposite, top*** The hob has less need than other areas to be next to storage. Opt for gas for better heat control. For safety, install cookers and hobs away from windows, unless they have a flame-failure device to cut the supply if needed.

***Opposite, bottom left*** Glazed cabinet doors suit ceramics and glass. A grand modern home might not have these in the kitchen at all, but in dining-room cabinets; however, in this open-plan Long Island residence they are in the kitchen in view of the media-cum-sitting room.

***Opposite, bottom right*** For kitchens, ergonomic ease of use is crucial. In this Hollywood home, cabinetry original to the late 1950s house conceals all newly devised kitchen storage.

# kitchens

The kitchen has the most expensive square footage in the home and must run smoothly. It is the most likely source of chaos unless well planned. There is a reason for selecting uniform flatwear, one make of saucepan and plates that stack well: attention to detail in selecting cooking tools can mean storage works fluidly. Gone are the days of cookie cutters and jam-making kits: the modern kitchen produces mainly savoury food, and expert chefs plan a meal's prep time at twenty minutes tops.

The best kitchens available now are hyper-designed by firms like Bulthaup, Minotti kitchens, Tsunami and Smallbone (for a country look), which cover all aspects. The ultimate, in my mind, is a stainless-based Bulthaup design finished in fruit wood (pear or apple).

When designing your kitchen, look first to the food storage area, which includes refrigerator, cupboards for dry food and a prep area. The cooking domain comes next, with oven and hob flanked by work surfaces where hot pans can be placed. Then comes the washing area: sink and dishwasher with cupboards nearby for storing crockery.

Good kitchen storage systems mean cooks and laymen can operate as if practising Tai Chi, in a graceful and ordered manner, one's centre of gravity not wavering for a moment.

***Right, top*** Architect Fred Collin has created a low-tech London kitchen for himself and his wife, nevertheless with a strict bank of laminated cabinets below the glass countertop. A counter should be a standard elbow height of 90 centimetres (36 inches), based on average Western height, except for delicate operations such as icing a cake, which require a higher surface.

***Right, bottom*** Consideration for kitchen materials means doing the homework, but quality materials matter for resale value as well as durability. Whether your storage cabinetry is MDF, melamine-covered chipboard or solid wood with stainless steel, ensure internal fixtures are metal, not plastic. Handles must also be sound.

***Far right*** Architect Stephen Roberts in Manhattan has slotted this "expression" of a kitchen between a dining room and sitting room. As there are no doors and the room is passed frequently, neatness is vital: all storage and preparation facilities are below waist height.

# DECORATIVE | detail

# accessories

Throughout *Attention to Detail* I hope we have, through photography and words, managed to dispel the assumption that the scrutiny of detail means taking a close look at the more nebulous bits and bobs we find arranged around the home. These are not really "details" at all: they are more the accessories. Even furniture can be an accessory to the well-designed home, acting as stand-alone sculpture (unless consciously built in or forming part of a "total work of art"). However, the minutiae of accessories, as much as the detail of the fundamentals, hold the clue to personalising a home.

While the structure of a home is indicative of how we see ourselves, it is the more decorative elements within that are the first indication to a visitor, a key to first impressions. The two sides of a personality – one's own perception and the perception of others – have to work in harmony, so that the whole does not appear schizophrenic (quirky rooms can give mixed messages; better to mix drinks than metaphors). If you want to create a "whole" from your home, which is strongly advised, build on the foundation and, as in life, allow the odd intrigue to surface if it comes naturally but do not create a string of surprises, or it will all end up looking look like fiesta time, which is too colourful for words and exhausting, although briefly amusing. (Try to bear this in mind when giving house gifts: they should be suited both to you as a person and to the recipient's home, rather than to you and your own home. This way you may enhance their lives with but an ounce of your essence, and the gift will end up well placed. And please, no vacation gifts, as your experience of a far-away country will never be the same as another's.) We all wear our hearts on our sleeves, but I do believe we should try to keep some of the personality hidden if we can – it can be teased out later through conversation.

At the same time, don't be afraid to be different in a consistent way, if this reflects who you are. The co-founder of *The Spectator* (an age-old publication), Joseph Addison, wrote in 1714, "There is sometimes a greater judgement shewn in deviating from the rules of art, than in adhering to them; and... there is more beauty in the works of a great genius who is ignorant of all the rules of art, than in the works of a little genius, who not only knows but scrupulously observes them."

Colour is the very first element we perceive when entering a room, hence our memory of, for example, "Nancy Lancaster's yellow drawing room", the "red dining room at The Connaught" or the "Blue Bar" at The Berkeley hotel, all of which are in London. If the space and lighting are sound, like engineering, they will not be noticed at all but will just work well. The furniture arrangement and selection always beg comment, followed by the fabric used for drapes (if reasonably ostentatious), texture and, depending upon the room's use, decorative artefacts too.

A room is filled and emptied during its years of life, and in a good room the architecture of volumes has already achieved some sort of perfection, the walls alone having the proper space and cadence. If a room is beautiful when empty, it should not only remain beautiful when filled but become more enchanting still.

# furniture

English dramatist Noël Coward's singular advice to actors is reported to have been, "Just say the lines and don't trip over the furniture." Well, set design is one thing, Coward's main fear possibly the flimsiness of the furniture as well as extra and unscripted comical effect, but real living is rather more tangible. In a well-organised home there should be imaginary but clear pathways around furniture and through rooms, with absolutely no chance of tripping.

Whether you choose eighteenth-century Hepplewhite from Salem, Massachusetts, or flat-pack from the 1940s, it is wise first to consider the scale of furniture in a room, easily accomplished using a floorplan, with paper cut-outs representing the furniture cut to scale and placed on it. Computer imaging is an advanced way to view a scheme in three dimensions, but the cutout method can help to eliminate disaster, and is a useful, less timely and less costly way of editing.

French contemporary-interiors doyenne Andrée Putman was once asked to design for a hotel dining room chairs with backs taller than the sitters' heads, to make them feel important. This is a fallacy, ridiculous for numerous reasons, and Putman rightly refused. High chair backs would mean less vision, an interrupted sight line across the room, and more potential clumsiness and ugliness, sitters diminutive in their presence. High chair backs, like overly hoisted pictures, are vulgar. Overscale furniture, which has grown proportionally, is another matter, but the overriding consideration when selecting furniture should be comfort. Addition of furniture is the final touch to what Mongiardino described as a "roomscape".

# tables & chairs

Tables and chairs need not form a matching set, but must sit comfortably together in shape and scale. Most dining chairs do not have arms – too cumbersome – although if they are custom-designed for a table, the maker will have ensured that they fit under the tabletop and sit together without jarring. Over-wide chair backs can also be a hindrance, leaving excessive space between seats and making it impossible to pull up an extra chair.

Table legs can cause all measure of problem too, hence the attraction of Eero Saarinen's 1950s "Tulip" table with its single-pedestal base. Gateleg tables may make space when folded but do no favours to human legs attempting to avoid their zigzag mechanics. A simple four-legged table, whether square, circular, oval or rectangular, where the legs fall directly from corners – or in the case of the circle or oval at equal intervals – is still the most accommodating for family or small dinner parties, since chairs can glide freely beneath.

***Previous page*** A country home need not be unkempt. In this American dining room, neutral colour palette and warm textures soften the straight lines of the hide-covered chairs.

***Above*** In the same home, kitchen table and chairs are Arts and Crafts English, well suited to the Shaker cabintery. The Shakers, an offshoot of the Quakers, created simple yet precise and delightful furniture.

***Right*** The 1950s chair in Italy changed appearance due to a byproduct from tyre manufacture: foam rubber. These 1950s chairs are mighty comfortable.

***Opposite*** I have not sat in a dining chair as comfortable as these, in Milan, for a long time: the pad is perfect, as is the height of chair in relation to table. Fabric, here with a utilitarian shiny coating, is also important for comfort and elegance.

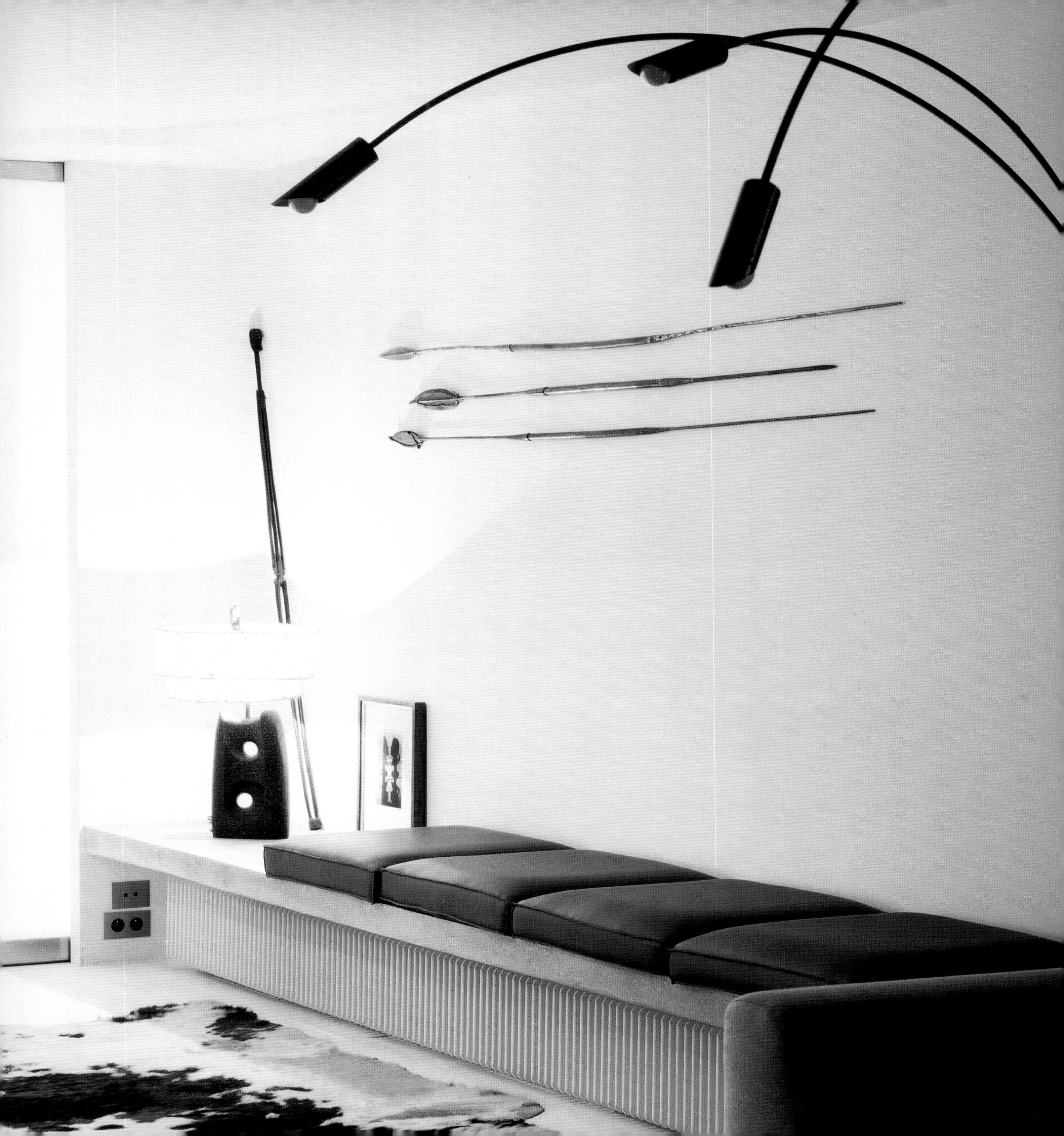

preserved at Knole in Kent (a house unaltered since 1603). These pieces exhibited the most advanced thinking of the time, and had arrived in the house via Frances Cranfield, daughter and heir to Lionel Cranfield, Earl of Middlesex. Besides being a power-hungry minister and Master of the Great Wardrobe, the Earl was connected to the Mercers' Company, and I think this has something to do with it. He and his daughter showed flair in producing sofas and chairs that were lower to the ground, with deep cushions: the sofas at Knole have adjustable ends and some of the chairs have adjustable backs.

The development of the sofa, incidentally, described at the time as an armchair extended laterally to seat two or more people, coincided with development of a light cane chair. In the seventeenth century, as in the twentieth, conservative living habits did not prevent development of new furniture to answer new needs. Ardent bibliophile Samuel Pepys even invented the first glazed bookcase in this era. The occasional table followed, all new elements creating an informality that filtered into structured lives.

***Opposite, top left*** The simple "club" armchair, a regular feature in 1940s French clubs (first appearing in the Deco salon), now adorns glamorous rooms the world over, despite its demure appearance. It is the most comfortable of chairs, deep enough to curl up in, pert enough to sit up in. It can evoke a kasbah feel too, and appears in French Moroccan schemes. Many firms make equivalents, but I prefer patina'd leather.

***Opposite, top right*** New York fashion prefects Badgley and Mischka devised the ultimate well-dressed chair: a vintage bedroom buttonback chair from Amalgamated Home, covered in raincoat nylon. Apparel-quality fabrics are not always appropriate for furniture upholstery.

***Opposite, bottom*** In this Sag Harbor house by architect Audrey Matlock, a pair of "Harry" chairs, from B&B Italia and designed by Antonio Citterio, hold the symmetry opposite a 1998 "Harry" sofa.

***Above left*** Charles and Ray Eames designed the "Aluminium Group" for indoor and outdoor domestic use but, although here in a domestic interior, the chair is now used pretty much exclusively in offices. An outstanding example of functionality in design and readily available in re-edition, it should remain in the domestic interior.

***Above*** Arne Jacobsen's "The Egg" chair (foreground in this scheme by Shelton and Mindel), a foam-upholstered moulded fibreglass shell seat on a swivelling cast-aluminium base, was developed in 1958 for the lobby of Copenhagen's Royal SAS Hotel. Jacobsen sought maximum comfort from minimum padding.

# soft furnishings

John Ruskin (1819–1900), British art critic, thinker and social commentator, particularly influenced Pre-Raphaelite painting in all its voluminous glory and predilection for detail. The Pre-Raphaelites' mission, to produce genuine art rooted in realism, was a reaction against formulaic Royal Academy art. Of fabric, Ruskin wrote, "Whole cloth is wool of sheep, thread of flax, bark of tree – there exists no matrix. It can be shaped beyond the boundaries of origin. It shifts from the potential to an actuality that has a myriad of shapes and a myriad of ways of moving, responding to the action of the individual who manipulates it. It possesses the mysterious sense of unaccountable life in things themselves." How right he was: cloth is both planar and pliable. It can be given volume, compressed, pleated (especially in a contemporary interior), or traditionally swagged and festooned. Cloth is ductile (it expands and contracts) and with its many guises can help both small and large architecture. Its potential is almost boundless, since it can be opaque or transparent, of different weights, densities, textures and dimensions.

Many designers and other stylish creatures think fabric old hat, but I disagree. Soft furnishings temper the beat of a room that is otherwise brittle, and at windows and doors offer protection from heat, sun and cold. Fabrics help a room's natural inclination to breathe, and absorb sound too.

My natural inclination is to consider cloth in the early stages of design: perhaps fabric-covered walls (in panels, the French way) might make a smart and textured or satin-smooth finish, the rest of the room retaining utter simplicity. Fabric is a welcome addition to a modern home and can be used in a multitude of ways without creating a bad pastiche.

# window treatments

Unless you are not overlooked, some attempt at a window treatment is advisable; few of us are blessed with an uninterrupted exterior space. As we have travelled more widely, window dressings have been adopted from far-flung places. Basic blinds originated in India, the festooned kind from Venice, and screens from the Orient, particularly Japan. Window dressings varied because of local materials as well as climates. In truth, in temperate climates we rarely need them for heat insulation, since we have sophisticated heating systems and in some cases double glazing (this is becoming less popular since it is difficult to keep clean, although it can be valuable for sound absorption) but they still have their place.

With curtains, as with pieces of jewellery, the most important point is that they should be well made and finished to perfection. It is attention to detail that gives a window covering quality. As interior designer Michael Greer said in *Inside Design*, "Labor to make

***Previous page*** Many interior designers custom-make rods of handforged iron or steel, but elegant modern solutions can be purchased off the shelf. A rod-and-eyelet system is appropriate for single unlined curtains.

***Opposite, far left*** With the right proportions, looped headings (metal rings) can be elegant as well as simple. They are particularly useful for a curtain in front of a radiator, as air can circulate.

***Opposite, top right*** These heavy silk double-lined pinch-pleated curtains are bordered with braid. The Roman blind gives extra protection. Deep pinch pleats look best on heavy full-length fabric.

***Opposite, bottom right*** The upper support of this Roman blind is imperceptible. If there is furniture in front of a window, choose an easily operated window treatment.

***Above*** In low-ceilinged rooms, curtains should lead the eye downward; pelmets and low-slung tiebacks may help. Here, diaphanous translucent fabric makes the windows seem larger.

proper curtains runs neck and neck with the cost of materials and sometimes exceeds it. But there is nothing to do but pay not pray, for poorly tailored curtains, like poorly tailored couturier originals, amount to a waste of fabric. 'Curtains' is the preferable term, but I sometimes lose my nerve and substitute 'draperies' (on the bill) – more substantial and important sounding – in estimates which might otherwise bring on a client apoplexy." In buying fabric for curtains, remember that hanging fabric is likely to stretch a little, so hems should be tacked up, and curtains hung for a few days before final hemming.

Greer was also reportedly the first to use the term "Roman" for horizontal concertina or accordian-fold fabric blinds, about which he commented, "Beyond the immaculate way they look, compelling recommendations for Roman shades are the facts that they can fall from ceiling to floor, can mask the architectural caprices... and can imply a window area – both in height and width – greater than exists." Hopefully a well-designed home has no caprices to disguise, but the point about visual enlargment is valid for many window treatments.

***Above*** Blinds have become very sophisticated indeed of late, and architects like Vincent Van Duysen dream of systems that glide freely at the touch of a button, as here. Some even move automatically according to the light.

***Right, above*** Plantation (interior) shutters originated in plantation houses. Most have fine louvres, but some are made from large panels of solid wood. In tall rooms, as here, poles must be used to tease and lift the louvres at a height.

***Right*** Paris fabric designer Dominique Kieffer has used double-faced interlined curtains dyed a beautiful shade that appears to have faded with time, although it has not. Fabric banners of different texture on adjacent walls unify the scheme through colour .

***Far right*** The chic combination of sensual, heavy silk taffeta curtains with gauzy sheer dark net offers four looks in one, with varying degrees of privacy, light and shimmering layered effect.

***Left*** Cushions not only soften the hardness of a chair, daybed or settee (sofas are generally plump enough) but bring incidental texture and accent colour. Piping adds definition. Like clothing accessories, cushions can be changed at whim.

***Below*** This combination – a band of expensive fabric on an otherwise plain cushion – is a way to keep costs down but standards up. Textile designers often make cushions as samples of their work.

***Right, top*** A fabric alone can provide inspiration for a cushion's form. These cushions on stools by a bed with sculptural taffeta cover are fringed with a modern stiff synthetic gauze.

***Far right, top*** Bold striped fabric covers cushions for a daybed. Small pattern and large pattern mixed together offers a more interesting blend than a combination of patterns that are all middle-sized.

***Right, bottom*** On this chocolate-fabric-covered bedhead, cushions add comfort. Modern bedrooms tend to look like hotel rooms, thanks to our growing experience of travel. For urbane chic at home, sophisticated fabrics may be coordinated with the furniture itself.

***Far right, bottom*** Cushions in the living room should always be firm; in the bedroom a less-stuffed goose-down pillow absorbs the shocks of the day.

# cushions

A cushion is a very ancient article of furniture, and inventories of the contents of great houses in the early Middle Ages constantly make mention of them. In those days a cushion was often leather-covered and of great size, firm enough to serve as a seat. It was indeed used as such in France and Spain following the Middle Ages, and for some years was regarded at the Spanish court as a peculiarly honourable chair substitute. In France, the right to kneel behind the king in church upon a cushion was both strictly regulated and jealously guarded. This type of cushion was called a *carreau* or square.

The tendency of all furniture since then has been to grow smaller, and the cushion is no exception. Today, cushions have covers that can be removed, so maintenance need not be too difficult and covers can be altered according to season. Not everyone needs or wants cushions, but they can be attractive and inspiring. Incidentally, the word "sofa" derives from the Arabic *suffah*, which is the cushion on a camel's saddle.

# art & ornament

In a 1945 interview, Pablo Picasso (1881–1973) said, "Painting is not made to decorate apartments. It's an offensive and defensive weapon against the enemy." He often talked of how painters and poets would not be expelled from society despite the danger they provoked.

Picasso was a hard worker. Take his sculptures in clay: in order to master working with slips, oxides and glazes, he took great risks technically, but discovered his own techniques of ceramic art, including methods of sgraffito (scratching through one colour to reach another) and wax resist. Over a period of twenty years, he fired some 3,500 clay objects, some good, others not so. Well, art is not created to decorate apartments; it is born from passion and a gamut of reactions. But we can at least attempt to resolve how best to display great works of art, and lesser pieces, in support of any artist's effort.

Many books teach how to group pictures, but to my mind all pictures, whether valuable or just admired, are "grouped", in that they sit together with other things. They may be paired (a diptych acts as one and must be displayed as such, a triptych too) but are rarely single, since any art form, unless in a room on its own, must be in relation to something else – even just the observer. So pictures and objects, en masse, are always grouped; "How grouped?" is the more relevant question.

Hanging groups of pictures successfully depends upon a sense of rhythm. With sculpture, any piece can appear as still life if given the right platform. A single piece has resonance, while two or three together should have harmony, and if you are going for more than three, just keep composing.

# fixed pieces

I see pictures and ornaments, mirrors too, as either "fixed" or "movable". This is not to say that the former cannot be changed around, but that they have been given a place of relative permanence where a bracket, nail or some kind of support has been applied to a surface for the picture to be hung in a predetermined manner or, for three-dimensional objects, given a plinth or shelf upon which to be displayed.

In the most seamless modern home, shadow gaps between wall faces and ceilings provide a lip on which to link hooks and thus suspend pictures from wires, strings and poles. Organised, precise multiple hanging can be very smart if a bold statement, but dull if pastel. Picture rails used to provide a similar means to hang hooks for pictures, but no longer suit the modern home since they tend to disrupt the internal scale of the room.

A fixed position means that lighting, natural or otherwise, can be designed to illuminate each item's finer features. Fixed objects tend on the whole to be more revered.

***Previous page*** Hung from a shadow gap, the art appears taut in suspension. Box frames add to the pristine drama. The walls remain untouched.

***Far left*** This niche, further defined by a wide painted border, is a stage upon which to display anything, a more permanent focal point than the objects displayed.

***Far left, below*** All manner of frames, thick and thin, dark wood and light, imbue a sense of mystery to a very personal collection of drawings and paintings. They are hung quite deliberately, in syncopated form, despite their haphazard appearance.

***Left, below*** In Paris, Dominique Kieffer's display is both masculine and feminine: banners of her fabric hung from poles break up a wall, warm the hallway, and create a surface on which to display art.

***Right*** Jamie Drake in New York has closed in his wall by a sequence of picture-frame sizes. Each piece of art is unique but the system repetitive. This display suits a connecting room: it can appear almost kinetic if studied for a long time.

***Below*** Collections of glass must be well lit, naturally or artificially. Mark Rios, in California, can rely on hillside sun to illuminate his green, yellow and blue glass, to glorious and refreshing effect.

***Below right*** A collection of disparate drawings by different artists, published by Mill Valley, California, is grouped in uniform frames. Contrasting yet linked, they hold the eye.

***This page*** This vast mirror leaning against the wall is a fairytale moment in a serious house, absolutely charming in its scale. It is probably safer not to hang such a large, heavy mirror, although with a steel bracket running its width and a high enough ceiling, it would be feasible.

***Opposite, top right*** Walls and ceilings are not always straight. You can spend a long time using a spirit level when hanging pictures, only to find it ineffective. A shelf solves the problem.

***Oppposite, bottom left*** The thin, tall mirror leans at an angle against the wall, while the extraordinary circular mirror and its light hang like clothing on a stand.

***Opposite, bottom right*** A shelf supporting art serves as a horizon line that brings together pictures of any dimension. Leaning pictures creates a relaxed vision and offers greater opportunity for change.

# movable pieces

Movable objects are not necessarily impermanent; on the contrary, they are often the most coveted decorative elements in a home (in some cases, the most held), and for this reason find a more accessible platform. Having a "hands-on" approach is currently seen as the healthiest pathway to modern nirvana, and in display, if an object or painting can readily be removed, moved or just picked up for interest's sake, then it surely must give pleasure.

In Edric Van Vredenburgh's antique-gallery-cum-home on London's Portobello Road, all manner of art and objects can be found, framed pieces resting against walls (it is hard to sell something that is firmly attached), others just "hanging out" in vague anticipation of discovery. Yesterday I picked up a heavy marble form there that just ached to be held. Attractively undesigned, it was randomly positioned with others on a mantelpiece. It turned out to be about three thousand years old, from Pakistan. For all the casual approach, these objects are resolutely cherished – as one's home should always be.

# DIRECTORY

## FLOORING AND SURFACES

***Abet Laminates***
70 Roding Road, London Industrial Park, London E6 4LS, UK
Tel: +44 (0)20 7473 6910
And at: 100 Hollister Road, NJ 07608, USA
Tel: +1 201 541 0701
www.abetlaminati.it
Leading manufacturers of high-pressure laminates.

***Amtico***
Kingfield Road, Coventry CB6 5AA, UK
Tel: +44 (0)121 745 0800 or +44 (0)800 667 766
www.amtico.com
Also at: 18 Hanover Square, London W1, UK
Tel: +44 (0)20 7629 6258
And: Suite 809m, The New York Design Center, 200 Lexington Avenue, New York, NY 10016, USA
Tel: + 1 800 291 9885
Fax: +1 212 545 8382
www.amtico.com
Replicate stone, wood, slate, glass, metal.

***Bisazza***
92-94 Church Road, Mitcham, Surrey, UK
Tel: +44 (0)20 8640 7994
www.bisazza.com
Mosaic tiles.

***Cast Advanced Concretes***
Unit 4 Rempstone Barns, Corfe Castle, Dorset BH20 5JH, UK
Tel: +44 (0)1929 480757

***Corian*** (surfaces)
Dupont Corian, Maylands Avenue, Hemel Hempstead, Herts HP2 7DP, UK
Tel: +44 (0)800 962 116
www.corian.com

***Domus Tiles***
1 Canterbury Court, 6 Camberwell New Road, London SE5, UK
Tel: +44 (0)845 062 5555
And at: 33 Parkgate, London SW11, UK
Tel: +44 (0)845 062 5555
www.domustiles.com, service@domustiles.com

***Falke Design***
Sweden
Tel: +46 (0)340 656 200
Fax: +46 (0)340 656 380
www.falckedesign.com
Durable wood and stone flooring from Sweden.

***Fired Earth***
Twyford Mill, Oxford Rd, Adderbury, Oxfordshire OX17 3HP, UK
Tel: +44 (0)1295 812088

***Forbo Linoleum***
UK
Tel: +44 (0)1592 647209
www.forbo-nairn.co.uk

***Formica Ltd***
Coast Rd, North Shields, Tyne and Wear NE29 8RE, UK
Tel: +44 (0)1912593000
www.formica-europe.com

***Lasco Flooring***
41 Maltby Street, London SE1, UK
Tel: +44 (0)20 7237 4488

***H & R Johnson***
Highgate Tile Works, High Street, Turnstall, Stoke-on-Trent, Staffs ST6 4JX, UK
And: Johnson USA Inc., PO Box 2325, Farmingdale, NJ 07727, USA
Ceramic tiles.

***Linestone Gallery***
Arch 47, South Lambeth Road, London SW8 1SS, UK
Tel: +44 (0)20 7735 8555

***Junkers***
Wheaton Court, Commercial Centre, Wheaton Road, Witham, Essex CM8 3UJ, UK
And: 4920 East Landon Drive, Anaheim, CA 92807, USA
Wooden flooring.

***Mosaic Workshop***
Unit B, 443-449 Holloway Road, London N7 6LJ, UK
Tel: +44 (0)20 7263 2997

***Paris Ceramics***
583 King's Road, London SW6 2EH, UK
Tel: +44 (0)20 7371 7778

***Rowi Parquet International***
PO Box 1033, 3430 BA Nieuwegein, Netherlands
Tel: +34 (0)2 60206
Fax: +34 (0)2 64174
www.rowi.nl

***Solid Floor***
53 Pembroke Road, London W11, UK
Tel: +44 (0)20 7221 9166

***Stone Age***
19–23 Filmer Road, London SW6 7BU, UK
Tel: +44 (0)20 7385 7954

***The Stone and Ceramic Warehouse***
51/55 Stirling Road, London W3 8DJ, UK
Tel: +44 (0)20 8993 5545

***UK Marble Ltd***
21 Nurcott Road, Hereford HR4 9LW, UK
Marble and granite flooring, panelling, fireplaces and mouldings.

***Turgön Hardwood Flooring***
91 Ballards Lane, Finchley, London N3 1XY, UK
And at: 955 Fulham Road, London SW6 5HY, UK
Tel: +44 (0)800 169 3743
www.turgon.co.uk, info@turgon.co.uk

***Worlds End Tiles***
British Rail Yard, Silverthorne Road, Battersea, London SW8 3HE, UK
Tel: +44 (0)20 7819 2100

## CARPETS

***Avena Carpets***
Bankfields Mill, Haley Hill, Halifax, West Yorkshire HXE 6ED, UK
Tel: +44 (0)1422 330261
Custom-made carpet.

***Crucial Trading***
The Plaza, 535 Kings Road, London SW10, UK
Tel: +44 (0)20 7376 7100

***Keshishian***
73 Pimlico Road, London SW1W 8NE, UK
TEL: +44 (0)207 730 8810
Quality antique rugs.

***Rama Carpets***
UK
Tel: +44 (0)20 8802 1010
sammy@ramacarpets.com

***Vorwerk***
Kuhlmannstrasse 11, D-31785 Hameln, Germany
Tel: +49 (0)5151 1030
www.vorwerk-carpet.com

***V'Soske Joyce UK Ltd***
The Clocktower, Coda Centre, Munster Road, London SW6 6AW, UK
Tel: +44 (0)20 7386 7200

***Wool Classics***
Chelsea Harbour Design Centre, 1st Floor, London SW10, UK
Tel: +44 (0)20 7349 0090

## WALLCOVERINGS

***Cole & Son***
G10 Chelsea Harbour Design Centre, Chelsea Harbour, London SW10
Tel: +44 (0)20 7376 4628
www.cole-and-son.com
Wallpapers.

***Tektura***
Tel: +44 (0)20 7536 3311
www.tektura.com, sales@tektura.com
Contemporary wallcoverings of varying materials.

***Jocelyn Warner***
Designtext, Blumenthal Showroom, D&D Building, 979 Third Avenue, New York, NY, USA
Tel: +1 212 752 2535
jocelyn@jocelynwarner.com
And: 19–20 Sunbury Workshop, Swanfield Street, London E2 7FL, UK
Tel: +44 (0)20 7631 4773
Wallpapers.

## PAINT

***Crown Paint***
Crown Berger Ltd, Crown House, PO Box 37, Holins Road, Darwen, Lancashire BB3 OBG, UK
Tel: +44 (0)870 240 1127
www.crownpaint.co.uk

***Designer Paint***
UK
www.designerpaint.co.uk
info@designerpaint.co.uk
Founded in 1995 by David Oliver and Sophie Grattan-Bellew, Paint & Paper Library is a paint and wallpaper company specialising in the design and supply of premium paint and wallpaper to the discerning.

***Dulux***
www.dulux.com

***Farrow & Ball***
Uddens Trading Estate, Wimborne, Dorset BH21 7NL, UK
Tel: +44 (0)1202 876141
And (London stockist): 249 Fulham Road, London
Tel: +44 (0)1202 876141

***John Oliver***
33 Pembridge Road, London W11 3HG, UK
Tel: +44 (0)20 7221 6466

**Paint Library**
London, UK
www.paintlibrary.co.uk
Further paint resource.

## DOOR FURNITURE

**Allgood plc**
297 Euston Road, London
NW1 3AQ, UK
Tel: +44 (0)207 387 9951
www.allgood.co.uk
Fine architectural ironmongery products.

**Crittal**
Crittall Windows Ltd,
Springwood Drive, Braintree,
Essex CM7 2YN, UK
Tel: +44 (0)1376 342106
Fax: +44 (0)1376 349662
www.crittall-windows.co.uk
hq@crittall-windows.co.uk
Manufacturers of Walter Gropius's Bauhaus windows and those for Frank Lloyd Wright's Falling Water. Quality steel windows since 1849.

**Gordon Watson**
UK
(See Furniture and Design Stores, page 219.)
Handmade handles and pulls.

**Technoline**
Lötzener Str. 2–4,
D-28207 Bremen, Germany
Tel: +49 (0)421 437350
Fax: +49 (0)421 4373525
info@tecnoline.de
Bauhaus door handles, including classic Modernist designs by Walter Gropius.

## WINDOW TREATMENTS

**The Shutter Shop**
Unit 2/8, Chelsea Harbour
Design Centre,
London SW10, UK
Tel: +44 (0)20 7351 4204

**Silent Gliss Ltd**
Star Lane, Margate, Kent
CT9 4EF, UK
Tel: +44 (0)1843 863 571
www.silentgliss.com
Contemporary window treatments, Roman blinds, shutters of all kinds.

**Warmerdams**
Cattlegate Rd, Crews Hill,
Enfield, London EN2 9DX, UK
Bespoke Curtains.

## HEATING

**Acova Radiators**
B15 Armstrong Mall,
Southwood Business Park,
Farnborough, Hants GU14,
UK
Tel: +44 (0)1252 531207
Fax: +44 (0)1252 531201
www.acova.co.uk

**Aestus**
Unit 5, Strawberry Lane
Industrial Estate,
Strawberry Lane, Willnehall,
West Midlands WV13, UK
Tel: +44 (0)1902 632256
www.aestus-radiators.com,
sales@aestus-radiators.com

**Bisque**
244 Belsize Road,
London NW6, UK
Tel: +44 (0)12 2547 8500
www.bisque.co.uk

**Caradon Stelrad**
PO Box 103, National
Avenue, Hull HU5, UK
tel: +44. (0)870 849 8056
www.stelrad.com
Radiators.

**CVO Firevault**
36 Great Titchfield Street,
London W1W 8BQ, UK
Tel: +44 (0)20 7580 5333
Fax: +44 (0)20 7255 2234
www.cvo.co.uk

**Myson Towel Warmers**
Emlyn Street, Farnworth,
Bolton, Lancs BL4, UK
Tel: + 44 (0)120 486 3200
www.mysontowelwarmers.co.uk,
sales@mysontowelwarmers.co.uk

**Norfolk Stoves**
Street Farmhouse, Fakenham
Road, Norwich, Norfolk
NR9 5SP, UK
Tel: +44 (0)1603 860762
Woodburning stoves.

**Platonic Fireplace Company**
Phoenix Wharf, Eel Pie
Island, Twickenham,
Middlesex TW1 3DY, UK
www.platonicfireplaces.co.uk
Tel: +44 (0)20 8891 5904
Fax: +44 (0)20 8892 2590
Owned and run by architect Henry Harrison. Modern and simple gas fires.

**Radiating Style**
Unit 15, Thompson Road,
Hounslow, Middlesex
TW3 3UH, UK
tel: +44 (0)870 072 3428
www.radiatingstyle.com,
sales@radiatingstyle.com.

**Thermocet**
www.thermocet.com
Woodburning stoves and a range of fireplaces and fires.

## LIGHTS

**Artemide**
92A Great Portland Street,
London W1, UK
Tel: +44 (0)20 7637 7238

**Patrice Butler**
10 Normandy Road, London
SW9 6JH, UK
Tel/Fax: +44 (0)20 7820 9796
Custom-made contemporary chandeliers; by appointment.

**ERCO**
38 Dover Street, London W1,
UK
Tel: +44 (0)20 7408 0320
www.erco.com
Uplighters and downlighters/ practical lighting for interior and exterior use.

**Foscarini**
Via delle Industrie 90/92,
Marcon 30020, Italy
Tel: +39 (0)4 1595 1199
www.foscarini.com

**The London Lighting Company**
135 Fulham Road,
London SW3, UK
Tel: +44 (0)20 7589 3612

**Luceplan**
Via E.T. Moneta 46,
Milano 20161, Italy
Tel: +39 (0)2 662 421
www.luceplan.it,
luceplan@luceplan.it

**Mathmos**
22-24 Old Street,
London EC1, UK
Tel: +44 (0)20 7549 7000,
www.mathmos.com

**Nessen**
420 Railroad Way, PO Box
187, Mamaroneck,
NY 19543, USA
Tel: +1 914 698 7799
Sleek designs.

**Louis Poulsen**
Louis Poulsen UK Ltd, Surrey
Business Park, Weston Road,
Epsom, Surrey KT17 1JG, UK
Tel: +44 (0)1372 848800
Fax: +44 (0)1372 848801
www.louis-poulsen.dk
louis.poulsen.uk@lpmail.com

**Produzione Privata**
www.produzioneprivata.it
Hand-blown lights by Michele de Lucchi.

**Pierre Scholtes Lighting**
Available from: ATEA
Lighting, 16 avenue
Stendhal, F-92140 Clamart,
France
Tel : +33 (0)1 41 36 07 70
Fax: +33 (0)1 41 36 07 80

**Tindle**
162 Wandsworth Bridge
Road, London SW6 2UQ, UK
Tel: +44 (0)20 7384 1485
Lampshades.

**Paul Verburg Ltd**
UK
Tel: +44 (0)20 7630 1257
lights@paulverburg.com
Custom-made modern lamps; by appointment

**David Weeks Lighting**
USA
(See Pucci International, page 216.)

## KITCHENS

**Alternative Kitchens**
9 Hester Road, London
SW11 4AN, UK
Tel: +44 (0)20 7228 6460

**Boffi**
www.boffi.com
Italy (See Major Furniture and Product Manufacturers, page 214.)

**Bulthaup**
37 Wigmore Street,
London W1, UK
tel: +44 (0)20 7317 6010

**Johnny Grey**
Fyning Copse, Rogate,
Petersfield, Hampshire
GU31 5DH, UK

**MFI**
UK (stores nationwide)
Tel: +44 (0)870 609555

**Poggenpohl Group UK** (trade)
Lloyd's Court, 681–685
Silbury Blvd Central, Milton
Keynes MK9 3AQ, UK
Tel: +44 (0)1604 763482

**Poliform**
278 King's Road, London
SW3 5AW, UK
Tel: +44 (0)20 7386 7600

**SieMatic**
Osprey House, Rookery
Court, Primett Road,
Stevenage, Herts SG1 3EE, UK
Tel: +44 (0)1438 369327

**Smallbone of Devizes**
220 Brompton Road, London
SW3 2BB, UK
Tel: +44 (0)20 7581 9989

**Tsunami**
27 Wigmore Street, London
W1U 1PN, UK
Tel: +44 (0)20 7408 2230

**Woodchester Cabinet Makers**
7 Bridge Street, Nailsworth,
Gloucestershire GL6 0AA, UK
Tel: +44 (0)1453 886411

## KITCHEN APPLIANCE SUPPLIERS

**AEG UK**
55-77 High Street, Slough,
Berkshire SL1 1DZ, UK
Tel: +44 (0)8705 350350

**Baumatic**
Baumatic Buildings,
6 Bennet Road, Reading,
Berkshire RG2 0QX, UK
Tel: +44 (0)118 933 6900

**Bosch Domestic Appliances**
Grand Union House,
Old Wolverton Road,
Wolverton, Milton Keynes,
Bucks MK12 5PT, UK
Tel: +44 (0)1908 328200

**Gaggenau (UK)**
Grand Union House,
Old Wolverton Road, Old
Wolverton, Milton Keynes,
Bucks MK12 5PT, UK
Tel: +44 (0)1908 328360

**Smeg (UK)**
Corinthain Court,

80 Milton Park, Abingdon, Oxon OX14 4RY, UK
Tel: +44 (0)870 990990

***Zanussi***
55-77 High Street, Slough, Berkshire SL1 1DZ, UK
Tel: +44 (0)8705 727727

## BATHROOMS

***Alessi***
22 Brook Street, London W1K 5DF, UK
Tel: +44 (0)20 7518 9091

***Alternative Plans***
UK
Tel: +44 (0)20 7228 6460
www.alternative-plans.co.uk

***Bathaus***
92 Brompton Road, London SW3 1ER, UK
Tel: +44 (0)20 7225 7620

***Bathstore.com***
410-414 Upper Richmond Road West, London SW14 7JX, UK
Tel: +44 (0)20 8878 2727

***Boffi***
(See Major Furniture Manufacturers, below.)

***CP Hart & Sons***
Newnham Terrace, Hercules Road, London SE1, UK
Tel: +44 (0)20 7902 1000
And at: 103–105 Regent's Park Road, London NW1, UK
Tel: +44 (0)20 7586 9856
www.cphart.co.uk

***Czech & Speake***
39c Jermyn Street, London SW1 Y 6DN, UK
Tel: +44 (0)20 7439 0216

***Edwins***
17,19 and 26 All Saints Road, London W11 1HE, UK
Tel: +44 (0)20 7221 3550

***Original Bathrooms***
143–145 Kew Road, Richmond, Surrey, UK
Tel: +44 (0)20 8940 7554
www.originalbathrooms.co.uk

***Slate World***
Westmoreland Road, Kingsbury Road, London NW9 9RN, UK
Tel: +44 (0)20 8204 3444

***Tsunami***
27 Wigmore Street, London W1U 1PN, UK
Tel: +44 (0)20 7408 2230

***West One Bathrooms***
45-46 South Audley Street, London W1, UK
Tel: +44 (0)20 7499 1845
And at: 41 Queenstown Road, London SW8, UK
Tel: +44 (0)20 7720 9333
www.westonebathrooms.com

## KITCHEN AND BATHROOM HARDWARE AND ACCESSORIES

***Aquasilia Products***
The Flyers Way, Westerham, Kent TN16 1DE, UK
Tel: +44 (0)1959 560000

***Aram Designs***
110 Drury Lane, London WC2B 5SG, UK
Tel: +44 (0)20 7557 7557

***Armatage Shanks***
Armitage, Nr Rugeley, Staffordshire WS15 4BT, UK
Tel: +44 (0)1543 490253

***Bath and Glass Works***
128 High Street, Hurstpoint, West Sussex BN6 9PX, UK

***Bathrooms International***
4 Pont Street, London SW1, UK
Tel: +44 (0)20 7838 7788
www.bathroomsint.com

***Brabantia***
Tel: +44 (0)12 8565 8844
www.brabantia.com
Kitchen accessories, bins, ironing boards.

***Burge & Gunson Ltd***
www.burgeandgunson.co.uk
Products by Dornbracht, Vola, Europbath, Hansgrohe, Perrin & Rowe, and Villeroy & Boch.

***Dornbracht***
Splash, 113 High Street, Cuckfield RH17 5JX, UK
Tel: +44 (0)1444 473355
Head office: Postfach 1454, Koebbingser Muehle 6, 5860 Iserlohn, Germany
www.dornbracht.com
World standards for bath fittings: European design with German craftsmanship.

***Franke*** (trade
Manchester International Office Centre, Styal Road, Manchester M22 5WB, UK
Tel: +44 (0)161 436 6280

***Grohe***
1 River Road, Barking, Essex IG11 0HD, UK
Tel: +44 (0)20 8594 7292

***HAF Designs***
HAF House, Mead House, Hertford, Herts SG13 7AP, UK
Tel: +44 (0)800 389 8821

***Hansgrohe***
Tel: +44 (0)870 770 1972
www.hansgrohe.co.uk

***Kitchen Ideas***
70 Westbourne Grove, London W2 5SH, UK
Tel: +44 (0)20 7229 3388

***Lucite Bowls***
Avante Bathroom Products, Unit K1 Thistle Way, Off Gildersome Spur, Gildersomee, Morely, Leeds LS27 7JJ, UK
Tel: +44 (0)113 244 5337

***The Majestic Shower Company***
1 North Place, Edinburgh Way, Harlow, Essex CM20 2SL, UK
Tel: +44 (0)1279 443644

***Matki***
Tel: +44 (0)1454 322888
www.matki.co.uk

***NewTeam Limited***
Brunel Road, Earlstrees Industrial Estate, Corby, Northants NN17 4JW, UK
www.newteamshowers.com

***Perrin & Rowe***
Orwell Close, Fairview Industrial Park, Rainham, Essex RM13 8UB, UK
Tel: +44 (0)1708 526361

***Teuco***
Suite 314, Business Design Centre, 52 Upper Street, London N1 0QH, UK
Tel: +44 (0)20 7704 2190
www.teuco.co.uk

***Volevatch***
France
Tel: +33 (0)1 55 78 22 40
www.volevatch.com, info@volevatch.fr

And at: 72 New Bond Street, London W1S 1RR, UK
Quality bathroom accessories used by uncompromising French interior designers.

## MAJOR FURNITURE AND PRODUCT MANUFACTURERS

***Alessi***
Omegna, Lake Orta, Italy
www.alessi.com
Founded: 1921
During the 1920s and 1930s, Giovanni Alessi produced copper, brass and nickel-silver tableware and household objects from his workshop. Since then the company has worked with Ettore Sottsass, Achille Castiglioni, Aldo Rossi, Massimo Morozzi, Philippe Starck, Jasper Morrison, Mark Newson, Ron Arad and Alessandro Mendini, who has also been design consultant since 1979. Alessi pans, cutlery and glassware are well known, as are their watches and bathrobes.

***B&B Italia***
Novedrate, near Milan, Italy
www.bebitalia.it
Founded: 1966
B&B has championed some of the best architects and designers of the day. Gaetano Pesce was an early designer; Jeffrey Bernett and Antonio Citterio followed suit. The London showroom, designed by John Pawson and Antonio Citterio, is a design destination in itself.

***Boffi***
Lentate, Como, Italy
www.boffi.com
Founded: 1934
Boffi is the Aston Martin of kitchen-design firms. It also creates bathroom accessories with the same seamless style. Designers and architects such as Sergio Asti, Luigi Massoni, Antonio Citterio, Piero Lissoni and Marc Sadler have created work for Boffi. Marcel Wanders's "Pipe" shower is a key recent Boffi piece. Boffi products can be found in museums such as MOMA in New York and the Louvre in Paris.

***Cappellini***
Aroso, Como, Italy
www.cappellini.it
Founded: 1946
Sub-brands: Cappellini Collezione, Mondo, Progetto Oggetto, Units
Founded by Giulio Cappellini, the company has an unrivalled reputation for fashionable, quality designs. Cappellini furniture is on permanent show in MOMA in New York and at the Pompidou in Paris. Both Jasper Morrison and the Bouroullec Brothers have created iconic designs for Cappellini.

***Driade***
Fossadello di Caoroso, Piacenza, Italy
www.driade.com
Founded: 1968
Sub-brands: DriadeStore, DriadeKosmo, Chef
A solid brand, with its flagship store in Milan, that began a kitchen design "Chef" in 1978. The whole range is regularly updated by designer Antonia Astori.

***Edra***
Perignano, Pisa, Italy
www.edra.com
Founded: 1987
Edra's pieces are thoroughly modern. The company has a history of promoting fresh talent. Its first collection, "I Nuovissimi", was a collaborative effort by young designers whose collections then went into production for the first time. More recently, the Campana brothers were also behind some great Edra pieces. Edra's art direction is in the hands of Massimo Morozzi.

***Flexform***
Meda, Milan, Italy
www.flexform.it
Founded 1959
Romeo, Pietro and Agostino formed Figli di Giovanni Galimberti to produce lacquered and upholstered furniture. The company, known today as Flexform, is now in the hands of their sons. Designers such as Antonio Citterio have contributed sofas, chairs and occasional tables.

***Flos***
Bovezzo, Brescia, Italy
www.flos.net
Founded: 1962
Sub-brand: Arteluce
Along with Artemide, Flos is a highly desirable lighting brand, originally set up by Arturo Eisenkeil, Dino Gavina and Cesare Cassina. Brothers Achille and Piergiacomo Castiglioni designed the company's first lamps – Arco, Relemme, Toio and Taccia – all became classics of Italian industrial design. Flos still signs up new talent today.

***FontanaArte***
Corsico, Milan, Italy
www.fontanaarte.com
Founded: 1932
Founded by Gio Ponti, architect and founder of *Domus* magazine. The pieces produced under Ponti are still highly covetable; FontanaArte continues to produce highly innovative work.

***Foscarini***
Marcon, near Venice, Italy
www.foscarini.it
Founded: 1981
Foscarini began life exploring the possibilities offered by Murano glass. Its use of both established designers and emerging talent continues to result in intriguing small-scale lights.

***Gaggenau***
Gaggenau, Karlsruhe, Germany
www.gaggenau.com
Founded: 1681
Gaggenau spells top-notch kitchen technology: for the best in appliances, we reach for a Gaggenau. It has its roots in an iron foundry founded by Margrave Ludwig Wilhelm von Baden in the 1700s. At one point it was turning out bicycles and motorbikes as well as kitchen equipment.

***Gallotti & Radice***
Cermenate, Como, Italy
www.gallottiradice.it
Founded: 1950s
As far back as the 1950s, Gallotti & Radice were experimenting with crystal in the design and production of furnishing. The firm has collaborated with the likes of Luigi Massoni, Andreas Weber, Davide Pizzigoni, Maurizio Duranti, Nanda Vigo, Carla Venosta, Gabriele Moscatelli and Italo Pertichini. Its vintage pieces and quirky mirrors are highly covetable.

***Georg Jensen***
Frederiksberg, Denmark
www.georgjensen.com
Founded: 1904
Georg Jensen, a silversmith and sculptor, had his beginnings in a workshop in Copenhagen. The company is now part of the Royal Scandinavia Group, and is known for its simple, stylish, traditional yet modern designs. Black cutlery forms part of its new range.

***Grohe***
Hemer, Westphalia, Germany
www.grohe.com
Founded: 1936
Grohe is known for its bathroom and kitchen fittings, from showers to taps, particularly Antonio Citterio's pieces. It prides itself on being the most prevalent fittings manufacturer in Europe and the largest exporter of bathroom fittings worldwide. The bathroom accessories are clean and chunky.

***Il Loft***
Gallarate, Milan, Italy
www.illoft.com
Founded: 1994
Il Loft was started by Giorgio Saporiti; all the furniture, fabrics and ceramic tiles are designed by Giorgio and his staff. If you want to add a curve to your life, Il Loft is the place to start. Its vast puffy curvilinear sofas are ideal for loafing loft dwellers.

***Kvadrat***
Ebeltoft, Denmark
www.kvadrat.dk
Founded: 1968
Sub-brand: Fanny Aronsen
Founded by Poul Byriel and Erling Rasmussen, Kvadrat is a specialist in upholstery and curtaining. The company focuses on contract and the upper retail market, with production in 28 textile factories and printworks in Western Europe. Its old fabrics are frequently reissued – recently spotted: some great Alexander Girard reproductions.

***Living Divani***
Brianza, Italy
www.livingdivani.it
Founded: 1969
Living Divani began as an armchair and sofa manufacturer. Located between Como and Milan, today it exports 75 percent of its work. The company's designer, Piero Lissoni, collaborates also with Boffi Cucine, Cappellini and Cassina. Lissoni's pieces are rarely lavish but always practical, bold in colour and perfectly proportioned.

***Luceplan***
Milan, Italy
www.luceplan.com
Founded: 1978
Luceplan was founded by three architects: Riccardo Sarfatto, the son of lighting pioneer Gino Sarfatti; Paolo Rizzatto; and Sandro Severi (Alberto Meda has since joined them as a partner). The lighting designs show a spare aesthetic, but the technological forms are far from frigid and often combine with bold colours.

***Miele***
Gütersloh, Germany
www.miele.de
Founded: 1899
Sub-brand: Imperial
Miele was founded by Carl Miele and Reinhard Zinkann and is a family-owned, family-run company. It focuses on the production of domestic appliances, commercial equipment and superb built-in kitchens.

***Minotti***
Meda, Milan, Italy
www.minotti.it
Founded: 1950s
Minotti produces streamlined sofas, armchairs and divans. The company was set up by Alberto Minotti, and is still a family business, run by sons Roberto and Renato. Quality furniture in an extensive neutral colour palette.

***Molteni & C***
Giussano, Milan, Italy
www.molteni.it
Founded: 1930s.
Using lots of natural materials, Molteni has developed a range of day and night furniture, from chairs, tables and sofas to beds and wardrobes. Paola Navone's "St Germain Chair" is a new classic, and Patricia Urquiola's "Clip Bed" a rare example of superlative bed design.

***Moroso***
Cavalicco, Udine, Italy
www.moroso.it
Founded: 1950s
A fine Italian brand. Patricia Urquiola's "Fjord" range was an exceptional collection. Konstantin Grcic, Tom Dixon and Alfredo Haberli have also turned out some fantastic pieces for Moroso.

***Poliform***
Inverigo, Brianza, Italy
www.poliform.it
founded: 1942
Poliform offers system furniture, complete fitted units with gently gliding drawers. The craftsmanship is exceptional – such as Carlo Colombo's "Sintesi" design, part of the "Day" collection. The new range of lacquer cabinets indicates Poliform's prowess at finishes.

***Venini***
Murano, Venice, Italy
www.venini.com
Founded: 1921
In 1921 Venetian antiques dealer Giacomo Cappellin and lawyer Paolo Venini, with glass-making in his family, together conceived Venini. They based themselves in Murano so that they could focus on glass production. The company has recently branched into high-quality glass furniture.

***Zanotta***
Milan, Italy
www.zanotta.it
Founded: 1954
The company founded by Aureilio Zanotta is still a trendsetter. Internationally renowned architects and designers who've worked for it include Achille Castiglioni (responsible for some of the greatest furniture of the last century), Marco Zanuso, Ettore Sottsass, Joe Colombo, Werner Asslinger and Ross Lovegrove. 1989 saw the Zanotta Edizioni collection of limited-edition pieces. The carbon-fibre "Fly Chair" by Mark Robson can be hung on the wall.

## FURTHER FURNITURE MANUFACTURERS

***Baker Furniture***
PO Box 1887, Grand Rapids, MI 49501, USA
Tel: +1 800 59BAKER
www.bakerfurniture.com
Collections by Barbara Barry and others.

***Baker Knapp & Tubbs***
Suite 300, The New York Design Center, 200 Lexington Avenue, New York, NY10016, USA
Tel: +1 212 779 8810
Fax: +1 212 689 2827
Formal, transitional and casual American furniture; by appointment.

***California Closets***
Tel: +1 800 336 9195
(in USA and Canada)
www.calclosets.com
Custom solutions for storage.

***Cassina SpA***
1, via L. Busnelli, 1-20036
Meda, Milan, Italy
Tel: +39 (0)36 27 03 13
info@cassina.it
Designs by Cassina, Mackintosh, Frank Lloyd Wright, Gerrit Rietveld, Le Corbusier, Charlotte Perriand, Philippe Starck and others.

***Cyrus company (Italy)***
Via Mottarone 60, 21010
Verghera di Samarate (VA), Italy
Tel: +39 (0)331 224911
Fax: +39 (0)331 721136
www.cyruscompany.it
Store locations: Via Alessandria 3, Milano
Tel: +39 (0)2 8360299
And: Via Borgospesso 8, Milano
Tel: +39 (0)2 7602461
White and light modern furniture.

***E15***
e15 Design und Distributions GmbH, Hospitalstrasse 4, 61440 Oberursel, Germany
Tel: +49 (0)61 71 97 95 0
Fax: +49 (0)61 71 97 95 90
www.e15.com, e15@e15.com
Showroom: Bergman Interior Fashion Beauty, IFB GmbH, Kaiserstrasse 23, 60311 Frankfurt Main, Germany
Tel: +49 (0)69 2400 5840
Fax: +49 (0)69 2400 5844
www.bergman.de, bergman@bergman.de
New simple-line wooden furniture.

***Ecart International***
11 rue Saint Antoin, 75004 Paris, France
Tel: +33 (0)1 42 78 79 11
Re-editions of twentieth-century classics.

***Fritz Hansen A/S***
Allerodvej 8, 3450 Allerod, Denmark
Tel: +45 (0)86 55 44 15
Designs by Arne Jacobsen, Vico Magistretti, Hans Wegner and others.

***The Knoll Group***
105 Wooster Street, New York, NY 10012, USA
Tel: +1 212 343 4180
and: Knoll International Ltd
1 East Market, Lindsey Street, London EC1A 9PQ, UK
Tel: +44 (0)20 7236 6655
www.knoll.com
Designs by Marcel Breuer, Eero Saarinen, Ettore Sottsas, Mies van der Rohe.

***McGuire Furniture Company***
151 Vermont Street, San Francisco, CA 94103, USA
Tel: +1 800 662 4847
New streamlined furniture, throughout America.

***Herman Miller Inc.***
855 East Main Avenue, PO Box 302, Zeeland, MI 49464, USA
Tel: +1 800 851 1196
www.hermanmiller.com
Furniture by George Nelson, Vernor Panton and others.

***Missoni Home***
Italy
Tel: +39 (0)3 3195 0311
www.missonihome.com
UK agent: Interdesign UK Ltd, G30 Chelsea Harbour Design Centre, London SW10 0XE, UK
Tel: +44 (0)20 7376 5272
Fax: +44 (0)20 7376 3020

***Moooi***
Netherlands
Tel: +31 (0)7 6572 2070
www.moooi.com
Small modern collection of innovative lights and furniture.

***Néotu***
25 rue du Renard, 75004 Paris, France
Tel: +33 (0)1 42 78 91 83
and: 409 West 44th Street, New York, NY 10036, USA
Tel: +1 212 262 9250
www.neotu.com
Contemporary furniture, soft furnishings and rugs, in limited editions.

***Niedermaier***
400 Notrh Oakley Boulevard, Chicago, IL 60612, USA
Tel: +1 312 4929400
www.niedermaier.com
Manufacturers of modern furniture, with designers such as Vicente Wolf.

***Poltrona Frau***
Germany
Tel: +44 (0)20 7336 6747
www.poltronafrau.it
High-quality leather and natural materials for seating. Collections created with Gio Ponti and Marco Zanusso.

***Pucci International***
44 West 18th Street, 12th Floor, New York, NY 10011, USA
Tel: +1 212 633 0452
Re-edition Eileen Gray rugs and items by Olivier Gagnère and Chris Lehreche and others; by appointment only.

***Thonet GmbH***
PO Box 1520, 3558 Frankenberg, Germany
Tel: +49 (0)64 51 50 80
Designs by Alvar Aalto and Marcel Breuer.

***Vitra AG***
13 Grosvenor Street, London W1X 9FB, UK
Designs by Charles Eames, Vernor Panton, Jaspar Morrison, Michele de Lucchi and Ron Arad.

## FABRIC

***Abbott and Boyd ltd***
8 Chelsea Harbour Design Centre, Chelsea Harbour, London SW10 0XE, UK
Tel: + 44 (0)20 7351 9985

***Borderline***
Unit 7, 2nd Floor, Chelsea Harbour Design Centre, London SW10 0XE, UK

***Borovicks Fabric***
16 Berwick Street, London W1, UK
Tel: +44 (0)20 7437 2180

***John Boyd Textiles Ltd***
Higher Flax Mills, Castle Cary, Somerset BA7 7DY, UK
Tel: +44 (0)1963 350451
Fax: +44 (0)1963 351078
www.johnboydtextiles.co.uk
Traditional and modern horsehair fabric.

***Britex Fabrics***
146 Geary Street, San Francisco, CA 94108, USA
Tel: +1 415 392 2910
Fax: +1 415 392 3906
www.britexfabrics.com
An entire world of fabrics under one roof.

***Chase Erwin***
Head Office: River House, 53 Lydden Grove, London SW18 4LW, UK
Tel: +44 (0)20 8875 1222
Fax: +44 (0)20 8875 1444
Silks, both plain and patterned.

***Dominique Kieffer***
(See Interior Designers and Architects, page 220.)

***Donghia***
485 Broadway, New York, NY 10013, USA
Tel: +1 212 925 2777
Fax: +1 212 925 4819
And:
Grüner Sand 51, D-32107 Bad Salzuflen, Germany
Tel: +49 (0)5222 91290
Fax: +49 (0)5222 912946
And:
G/23 and 2/21 Chelsea Harbour Design Centre, London SW10 0XE, UK
Tel: +44 (0)20 7823 3456
Fax: +44 (0)20 7376 5758
www.donghia .com
Chic modern fabric and furniture.

***Edelman Leather***
Tel: +1 800 886 TEDY (in USA and Canada)
Leather specialists.

***Howe Leather and Fabrics***
93 Pimlico Road, London SW1W 8PH, UK
Tel: +44 (0)20 7730 7987
Fax: +44 (0)20 7730 0157
Leather, fine linens, cottons.

***Kvadrat***
62 Princedale Road, London W11, UK
Tel: +44 (0)20 7229 9969
www.kvadrat.dk, kvadrat@kvadrat.co.uk

***Larsen***
Decoration & Design Building, 979 Third Avenue, New York, NY 10022, USA
Tel: +1 212 753 4488
Showroom.
And: 111 Eighth Avenue, Suite 930, New York, NY 10011, USA
Tel: +1 212 647 6901
Contemporary classics.

***Monkwell (head office)***
10-12 Wharfdale Road, Bournemouth, Dorset BH4 9BT, UK
Tel: +44 (0)1202 762456
Fax: +44 (0)1202 762582
www.monkwell.com

***Sahco Hesslein***
G/24 Chelsea Harbour Design Centre, Chelsea Harbour, London SW10 0XE, UK
Tel: +44 (0)20 7352 6168
Fax: +44 (0)20 7352 0767
And: Sahco Hesslein – Bergamo Fabrics, Decoration & Design Building, 979 Third Avenue, 17th floor, New York, NY 10022, USA
Tel: +1 212 888 3333
Fax: +1 212 888 3837
And: Sahco Hesslein United Arab Emirates, PO Box 26604, Dubai
Tel: +971 4 329179
Fax: +971 4 329142
www.sahco-hesslein.com
Modern designer fabrics for all uses.

***Scalamandré***
942 Third Avenue, New York, NY 10022, USA
Tel: +1 800 932 4361(for showroom locations)
Fine fabrics and trim.

***J Robert Scott***
2nd Floor, Unit 19, Chelsea Harbour Design Centre, Chelsea Harbour, London SW10, UK
Tel: +44 (0)20 7376 4705

***Zimmer & Rohde***
Unit 15, Chelsea Harbour Design Centre, London SW10 0XE, UK
Tel: +44 (0)20 7351 7115

## TRIM

***Wendy Cushing Trimmings***
G7 Chelsea Harbour Design Centre, London SW10 0XE, UK
Tel: +44 (0)20 7351 5796

***Wemyss Houlès***
40 Newman Street, London W1P 3EA, UK
Tel: +44 (0)20 7255 3305

## BED LINEN

***Frette***
98 New Bond Street, London W1, UK
Tel: +44 (0)20 7629 5517

***Gayle Warwick***
UK
At Thomas Goode (see page 218).

## ARCHITECTURAL SALVAGE

***Crowther of Syon Lodge***
Busch Corner, London Road, Isleworth, Middlesex TW7 5BH, UK
Architectural components and statuary.

***Materials Unlimited***
2 West Michigan Avenue, Ypsilanti, MI 48197, USA
New and reclaimed architectural materials, and antiques.

***Retrouvius***
32 York House, Upper Montagu Street, London W1H 1FR, UK
Tel: +44 (0)20 7724 3387
By appointment only.

## FURNITURE AND DESIGN STORES (BY COUNTRY)

***AUSTRALIA***

***Euroluce Lighting***
99 Flinders Street, Darlinghurst, Sydney
Tel: +61 (0)2 9380 6222
Flos, Luceplan, Nemo, Vibia and others.

***House of Balscheit***
1–3 Inkerman Street, St Kilda, Melbourne
Tel: +61 (0)3 9593 8744
Furniture and decorative art from the 1950s to 1970s.

***BELGIUM***

***Appart***
Museumstraat 50, B2000 Antwerp
Tel: +32 (0)3 260 96 96
www.appart.be
Interiors and furniture including Van Duysen's.

***In Store***
rue Tenbosch 90/92, Brussels
Tel: +32 (0)2 344 9637
www.instore.be
B&B Italia, Flexform, Poliform, Gaggenau, Gallotti & Radice, Grohe.

***Surplus***
Zwartezustersstraat 9, Gent
Tel: +32 (0)92 235 294
Contemporary international and local design.

***Tom Ravelingien***
Nieuwpoort 7, Gent
Tel: +32 (0)92 337 182
Lanterns, seating and screens; 1950s–1970s designs from Belgium, the Netherlands and Scandinavia.

***CANADA***

***Inform Interiors***
97 Water Street, Vancouver
Tel: +1 604 682 3868
www.informinteriors.com
Brands from Edra to Living Divani. Also in Seattle.

***Metropolitan Home***
450 West Hastings Street, Downtown, Vancouver
Tel: +1 604 681 2313
www.transport01.com/methome/flash.html
Vintage postwar designs and Scandinavian pieces from the 1950s and 1960s.

***Mod to Modern***
3712 Main Street, SoMa, Vancouver
Tel: +1 604 874 2144
"Rec-room chic" 1960s–1980s: clothing, furniture, collectables and accessories.

***CHILE***

***Opendark***
San Sebastián 2839, Las Condes, Santiago
Tel: +56 (0)2 373 7100
www.opendark.cl
Imported Flos and others from Italy, as well as Spanish and Argentinian lighting.

***DENMARK***

***Casa Shop***
Store Regnegade 2, Copenhagen
Tel: +45 3332 7041
www.casagroup.dk
Zanotta, Edra, Flexform and Minotti, as well as EIS, Fritz Hansen and La Palma.

***Georg Jensen Damask***
Dieselvej 1, DK-6000 Kolding
Tel: +45 7552 2700
www.georgjensen-damask.dk,
gjd@georgjensen-damask.dk
Classic Danish flatwear and dining accessories.

***FRANCE***

***Colette***
213 rue Saint-Honoré, Paris 1er
Tel: +33 (0)1 55 35 33 90
Destination boutique for lovers of high design.

***Galerie Yves Gastou***
12 rue Bonaparte, 75006 Paris
Tel: +33 (0)1 53 73 00 10
European 1930s and 1940s furniture and objects.

***Galerie Chastel Maréchal***
5 rue Bonaparte, 75006 Paris
Tel: +33 (0)1 40 46 82 61
French 1930s and 1940s furniture and objects.

***Modénature***
Créations Henry Becq, 3 rue Jacob, 59 rue de Seine, 75006 Paris
Tel: +33 (0)1 53 10 31 70
Tel: +33 (0)1 53 10 31 79
www.modenature.com
info@modenature.com
Wenge and other woods with soft, natural seating. Streamlined interior pieces, furniture and lights.

***Jérôme Abel Seguin***
36 rue Etienne Marcel, 75002 Paris
Tel: +33 (0)1 42 21 37 70
Hand-carved wooden artefacts from Indonesia.

***Galerie Vallois***
41 rue de Seine, 75006 Paris
Tel: +33 (0)1 43 29 50 84
Fine French early-to-mid-twentieth-century furniture.

***GERMANY***

***Dopo Domani***
Kantstrasse 148, Berlin
Tel: +49 (0)30 882 22 42
www.dopo-domani.com
B&B Italia, Minotti, Boffi's "Serie Square" bathroom range by Piero Lissoni, as well as Vitra, MDF, Braque.

***Förster & Hahn***
Osterstrasse 31, Hannover
Tel: +49 (0)51 13 06 81 88
Stockist of B&B Italia.

***Franta***
Maastrichterstrasse 18, Cologne
Tel: +49 (0)221 528 855
www.franta.de
Mid-twentieth-century furniture, trinkets and Scandinavian design.

***GREECE***

***Deloudis John***
217 Kifisias Ave, Marousi-Athens
Tel: +30 (0)80 69 094
Numerous brands, including B&B Italia, Flexform, Magis, FontanaArte, Flos, Living Divani, Driade and Cappellini.

***ISRAEL***

***Tollman's***
3 Hamenofim Street, Herzelia Pituach, Tel Aviv
Tel: +972 (0)9 956 2218
Minotti, Cassina, Cappellini, Alessi, Edra, Kvadrat fabrics, and Molteni.

***ITALY***

***B&B Italia Store***
via Durini 14, Milan
Tel: +39 (0)2 76 44 41
www.bebitalia.it
B&B's flagship store.

***Novelli Arredamenti***
Piazza Amedeo 21/22, Naples
Tel: +39 (0)81 41 32 33
www.novelliarredamenti.com
Driade and Alessi, along with Bulthaup kitchens.

***Ultramobile***
Via della Resistenza, 61030 Calcinelli Di Saltara
Tel: +39 (0)7 2187 8531
www.ultramobile.it,
info@ultramobile.it
Fantasic furniture by architect greats and designers.

***JAPAN***

***B&B Italia Osaka – Casa Mia Osaka***
3-5-7 Honmachi, Chuo-ku, Osaka
Tel: +81 (0)6 6271 8899
www.bebitalia.co.jp

***D & Department***
Tokyo Store, 8-3-2 Okusawa, Setagaya-ku, Tokyo
Tel: +81 (0)3 5752 0120
www.d-a-m.co.jp/depart
A cult department store that recycles discarded goods.

***KUWAIT***

***Villa Moda***
Free Trade Zone, Shuwaikh
Tel: +965 240 4814
Many big names, including Cappellini.

***LATVIA***

***Vincent Inspira***
K Ulmana Gatve 114/2, Riga
Tel: +371 750 0400
Stockist for Cappellini, Alessi, B&B Italia, Flos, FontanaArte, Foscarini, Gaggenau, Luceplan, Miele and Zanotta.

***MEXICO***

***Chic By Accident***
Colima 180, Col Roma, Mexico City
Tel: +52 (0)5 514 5723
www.chicbyaccident.com
American retro classics, from sofas to home accessories.

***Adriana Cruz De Cossio***
Mexico City
Tel: +52 (0)5 554 6969

***NETHERLANDS***

***Bebob Design Interior***
Prinsengracht 764, Amsterdam
Tel: +31 (0)20 624 5763
www.bebob.nl
Vitra and Philippe Starck's chair for Driade; collectables, new and secondhand.

***Frozen Fountain***
Prinsengracht 629, Amsterdam
Tel: +31 (0)20 622 9375
www.frozenfountain.nl
Local and international.

***NEW ZEALAND***

***Italy and Kitchens***
11 Teed Street, Newmarket, Auckland
Tel: +64 (0)9 529 4106
www.italyandkitchens.co.nz
Boffi and Binova.

***Matisse***
99 The Strand Parnell, Auckland
Tel: +64 (0)9 302 2284
www.matisse.co.nz
Stockists of B&B Italia, Moroso, Maxalto and MDF.

***FINLAND***

***Helsinki Ostaa Ja Myy***
Annankatu 5, Helsinki
Finnish and Danish classics; originals by Gio Ponti, Arne Jacobsen and Alvar Aalto.

***POLAND***

***MM Idea***
ul Zelazna 54, Warsaw
Tel: +48 (0)22 654 5530
www.mmidea.pl
Many of the big brands.

***PORTUGAL***

***Bastidor***
rua Passeo Alegre 694, Porto
Tel: +351 22 619 7620
Boffi, Cappellini, Flexform and Italian designs.

***SINGAPORE***

***Space Furniture***
Millenia Walk, 9 Raffles Boulevard, Singapore

Tel: +65 6416 0000
A good-looking store: B&B Italia, Driade and Zanotta.

***SOUTH AFRICA***

***IDSolutions***
170 Buitengracht Street, Cape Town
Tel: +27 (0)21 422 3800
And at: 39 Sloane Street, Bryanston, Johannesburg
Tel: +27 (0)11 706 2187
www.idsolutions.co.za
Amat3, Magis, Presotto and Frezza.

***Twiice International***
5 Winchester Road, Holland House, Parktown, Johannesburg
Tel: +27 (0)11 727 8800
www.twiice.com
Vitra and B&B Italia; also Driade, Ahrend and Arx.

***SPAIN***

***Vinçon***
Passeig de Gràcia 96, Barcelona
Tel: + 34 93 215 6050
www.vincon.com
Select modern furniture, accessories and homeware.

***SWEDEN***

***Jacksons***
Sibyllegatan 53, Stockholm
Tel: +46 (0)8 665 3350
www.jacksons.se
Vintage twentieth-century design and decorative arts.

***Orrefors***
www.orrefors.com, info@orrefors.se
Exquisite Swedish modern glass, vases and accessories, by Gunilla Allard, Lars Hellsten and Jan Johansson.

***Svenssons I Lammhult***
Järntoroget 2, Gothenburg
Tel: +46 (0)31 24 24 05
www.svenssons.se
Moroso, Flos and Luceplan, as well as Cassina, Artek, Louis Poulsen, Swedese, Zlamp.

***SWITZERLAND***

***Form 30 50 60***
Forchstrasse 179, Zurich
Tel: +41 (0)1 383 4336
Swedish designers, collectors' items and 1950s and 1960s originals.

***Luthi & Riccio***
15 rue Adrien-Lachenal, Geneva
Tel: +41 (0)21 601 0188
Stockists of Cappellini.

***UK***

***Alessi***
22 Brook Street, London W1
Tel: +44 (0)20 7518 9091
www.alessi.it, info@alessi.it

***Altfield***
Chelsea Harbour Design Centre, Unit 2/22, London
Tel: +44 (0)20 7351 5893
enquiries@altfield.com, www.altfield.com
Decorative accessories.

***Aram Store***
110 Drury Lane, London WC2
Tel: +44 (0)20 7557 7557
www.aram.co.uk
Contemporary furniture, lighting and accessories. The only UK licence for Eileen Gray designs, also stocks "Barcelona" furniture by Mies van der Rohe.

***Armani Casa***
37 Sloane Street, London SW1
tel: +44 (0)20 7235 6232
www.armanicasa.com
Armani's home collection.

***Atomic Antiques***
125 Shoreditch High Street, London, E1 6JE
Tel: +44 (0)20 7739 5923
An unusual mix of antiques.

***B&B Italia London***
250 Brompton Road, London SW3 2AS
Tel: +44 (0)20 7591 8111
A showroom designed by John Pawson and Antonio Citterio highlights the best of contemporary collections.

***Baccarat***
37 Old Bond Street, London W1
Tel: +44 (0)20 7409 7767
The ultimate in contemporary crystal chandeliers and glassware.

***Bowles & Linares***
32 Hereford Road, London
Tel: +44 (0)20 7229 9886
Contemporary furniture and unusual lights and lamps.

***Century***
68 Marylebone High Street, London W1 3AQ
Tel: +44 (0)20 7487 5100
Predominantly American classics from the 1950s.

***Chaplins***
17–18 Berners Street, London W1
Tel: +44 (0)20 7323 6552
www.chaplins.co.uk
Also at: 477–507 Uxbridge Road, Hatch End, Pinner, Middlesex HAA5
Tel: +44 (0)20 8421 1779
Cappellini and the best in other contemporary furniture.

***Coexistence***
288 Upper Street, London N1
Tel: +44 (0)20 7354 8817

***Ciancimino Ltd***
99 Pimlico Road, London SW1W 8PH
Tel: +44 (0)20 7730 9950
Italian mid-century to modern and other pieces.

***The Conran Shop***
Michelin House, 81 Fulham Road, London, SW3
Tel: +44 (0)20 7589 7401
Everything for the modern home.

***CVO Firevault***
36 Great Titchfield Street, London W1W 8BQ
Tel: +44 (0)20 7580 5333
Fax: +44 (0)20 7255 2234
www.cvo.co.uk

***Dallas & Dallas***
18 Montrose Street, Glasgow
Tel: +44 (0)141 552 2939
www.dallasanddallas.com
Contemporary furniture and design: Flos, Foscarini, Citterio and Luceplan for the home; Vitra and others for work.

***Driade***
Fourth Floor, Selfridges, 400 Oxford Street, London W1
tel: +44 (0)20 7318 3101

***Gallery 25***
26 Pimlico Road, London SW1
Tel: +44 (0)20 7730 7516
Continental mid-twentieth-century furniture, rare pieces and unknown provenance.

***General Trading Company***
144 Sloane Street, London, SW1
Tel: +44 (0)20 7730 0411
Quality sheets, bedlinens and home accessories.

***David Gill Galleries***
60 Fulham Road, London SW3 6HH
Tel: +44 (0)20 7589 5946
And: 3 Loughborough Street, London SE11 5RB
Tel: +44 (0)20 7793 1100
One-off contemporary and decorative furniture, objects, carpets by Fort Street Studio.

***Thomas Goode***
19 South Audley Street, London W1
Tel: +44 (0)20 7499 2823.
Glassware, crockery, decorative objects: Baccarat, William Yeoman, Gayle Warwick linens.

***Guedroitz Gallery London***
24 Pimlico Road, London SW1W 8LJ
Tel: +44 (0)20 7730 3111
Fax: +44 (0)20 7730 1441
www.russianfurniture.co.uk, guedroitz@russianfurniture.co.uk
High-quality antique Russian furniture.

***Habitat***
208 Kings Road, London SW3
Tel: +44 (0)20 7351 1211

***Fritz Hansen***
20–22 Rosebery Avenue, London EC1
tel: +44 (0)20 7610 4196

***Harrods***
The Contemporary Gallery
87-135 Knightsbridge, London SW1X 7XL
Tel: +44 (0)20 7730 1234
www.harrods.com
Re-editions of contemporary classic furniture and lights.

***Hemisphere***
173 Fulham Road, London SW3 6JW
Tel: +44 (0)20 7581 9800
Fine French and Italian mid-twentieth century furniture.

***Interiors Bis***
60 Sloane Avenue, London SW3
Tel: +44 (0)20 7838 1104
Furniture with French flavour.

***Ligne Roset***
23–35 Mortimer Street, London W1
Tel: +44 (0)20 7323 1248
www.ligne-roset.com

***David Linley***
60 Pimlico Road, London SW1W 8LP
Tel: +44 (0)20 7730 7300
Fax: +44 (0)20 7730 8869
www.davidlinley.com
Off-the-peg and bespoke furniture and accessories.

***Morplan***
56–58 Great Titchfield Street, London W1
Tel: +44 (0)20 7636 1887

***Poliform***
278 Kings Road, London SW3
Tel: +44 (0)20 7368 7600
www.poliform.it
Seamless furniture systems for the home.

***Pruskin Gallery***
73 Kensington Church Street, London W8
tel: +44 (0)20 7937 1994.
An interesting array of vintage and peroid furniture.

***SCP***
135–139 Curtain Road, London EC2
Tel: +44 (0)20 7739 1869
Also at: Fourth floor, Selfridges, 400 Oxford Street, London W1
Tel: +44 (0)20 7318 3138
www.scp.co.uk
Chairs and furniture by masters like Philippe Starck.

***Selfridges***
400 Oxford Street, London W1
Tel: +44 (0)870 837 7377
An extensive contemporary furniture collection.

***Skandium***
72 Wigmore Street, London W1
Tel: +44 (0)20 7935 2077
Scandinavian design.

***Themes and Variations***
231 Westbourne Grove, London W11 25E
Tel: 020 7727 5531
www.themesandvariations.co.uk
Quality late-twentieth-century furniture and objects.

***Twentytwentyone***
274 Upper Street, London N1
Tel: +44 (0)20 7288 1996
www.twentytwentyone.com
Cappellini and others.

***Van*** (Edric Van Vredenburgh)
105 Portobello Road, London
W11 2QB
Tel: +44 (0)20 7727 2739
Unusual art items, antiques and artefacts.

***Vessel***
114 Kensington Park Road,
London W11
Tel: +44 (0)20 7727 8001
Extraordinary sculptural glassware.

***Viaduct Furniture***
1–10 Summer's Street,
London EC1R 5BD
Tel: +44 (0)20 7278 8456
www.viaduct.co.uk
Contemporary furniture and lighting. Driade and more.

***Vitra***
30 Clerkenwell Rd, London,
EC1
Tel: +44 (0)20 7608 6200
www.vitranews.com,
sales_uk@vitra.com

***Waterford & Wedgwood***
173–174 Piccadilly, London
W1J 9EL
Tel: +44 (0)207 437 0282
Glass and ceramic pieces for the discerning eye.

***Gordon Watson Ltd***
50 Fulham Road, London
SW3 6HH
Tel: +44 (0)20 7589 3108
Fine twentieth-century European furniture, and bespoke objects such as door handles by Paul Belvoir.

***USA***

***Jonathan Adler***
8125 Melrose Avenue, Los
Angeles, CA 90046
Tel: +1 323 658 8390
Adler's vision for the home: lamps, ceramics, cushions and imaginative accessories.

***Amalgamated Home***
19 Christopher Street, near
Sixth Ave, New York
Tel: +1 212 691 8695
Cheerful store for offbeat furniture and accessories.

***L'Art de Vivre***
978 Lexington Avenue, New
York, NY 10021
Tel: +1 212 734 3510
Eclectic furniture gallery.

***Bernhardt***
Bernhardt Design NY, 58
West 40th Street 3rd floor,
New York, NY 10018
Tel: +1 212 997 6600
www.bernhardtdesign.com
Classic and contemporary furniture, tables, chairs and sofas, by designers such as Ross Lovegrove.

***Blackman Cruz***
800 North La Cienega
Boulevard, Los Angeles, CA
90069
Tel: +1 310 657 9228
Fax: +1 310 657 9583
Eclectic twentieth-century furniture and artefacts, collated with a French eye.

***Louis Bofferding***
New York
Tel: +1 212 744 6725
Antiquarian; by appointment only.

***Diva Furniture***
1300 Western Ave, Seattle
Tel: +1 206 287 9992
www.divafurniture.com
B&B Italia and Cappellini blend with Maxalto, Minotti, Fontana Arte, Venini, Flos, Alessi, Flexform, Luceplan.

***Dune***
88 Franklin Street, TriBeCa,
New York
Tel: +1 212 925 6171
www.dune-ny.com
Sleek furniture and accessories from cunning designers, including creative director Nick Dine.

***Furniture Co***
818 Greenwich Street, New
York, NY 10011
Tel: +1 212 352 2010
Select and refined modern furniture, ceramics and glass.

***Holly Hunt Ltd***
(Chicago, Miami,
Minneapolis, New York and
Washington DC )
Tel: +1 312 329 5999
Fax: +1 312 258 9513
Interior furnishings, lighting and textiles.

***Koo de Kir***
34 Charles Street, Boston
Tel: +1 617 723 8111
www.koodekir.com
Contemporary work from Moooi, Paolo Linti and US lighting designer Pablo.

***Limn***
290 Townsend Street, San
Francisco
Tel: +1 415 543 5466
Also at: 501 Arden Way,
Sacramento, CA
Tel: +1 916 564 2900
www.limn.com
1,200 manufacturers.

***Modernica***
57 Greene Street, New York
Tel: +1 212 219 1303
www.modernica.net
Re-edition classics: chairs by Eames, lamps by Nogichi, as well as own lines.

***Moss***
146/150 Greene Street, New
York
Tel: +1 212 226 2190
Select contemporary and American pieces from Edra, Zanotta, Flos and others. Re-edition tableware, glassware.

***NotNeutral Inc.***
6824 Melrose Avenue, Los
Angeles, CA 90038
Tel: +1 800 270 6511
Fax: +1 800 270 6544
www.notneutral.com
Ceramics, accessories and furniture.

***Liz O'Brien***
800A Fifth Avenue, New
York, NY 10021
Tel: +1 212 755 3800
Mid-twentieth-century American furniture.

***Pranich & Associates – The Wicker Works***
Suite 1520, Decoration and
Design Building, 979 Third
Avenue, New York,
NY 10022
Tel: +1 212 980 6173
Contemporary furniture in wicker and hemp.

***Retro Gallery***
524 1/2 North La Brea
Avenue, Los Angeles,
CA 90036
Tel: +1 323 936 5261
Fax: +1 323 936 5262
Retro furniture.

***J. Robert Scott***
Suite 220, Decoration &
Design Building, 979 Third
Avenue, New York ,
NY 10022
Tel: +1 212 755 4910
Fax: +1 212 755 4957
Furniture and fabric designs by Sally Sirkin Lewis.

***Twentieth***
8057 Beverly Boulevard, Los
Angeles, CA 90048
Tel: +1 323 904 1200
Twentieth-century furniture.

***Wyeth***
315 Spring Street, New York,
NY 10013
Tel: +1 212 243 3661
Vintage/ interesting objects.

## PLACES OF INTEREST

***Brooklyn Museum***
200 Eastern Parkway,
Brooklyn, NY 11238-6052,
USA
Tel: +1 718 638 5000

***Centraal Museum Utrecht***
Agnietenstr. 1, Postbus 2106,
3500 GC Utrecht,
Netherlands
Tel: +31 (0)30 362362

***Christie's***
8 King Street, London SW1,
UK
Tel: +44 (0)20 7389 2982
www.christies.com,
info@christies.com

***Alan Cristea Gallery***
31 Cork Street, London W1,
UK
tel: +44 (0)20 7439 1866
www.alancristea.com

***Le Corbusier/Villa Savoye***
82 rue de Villers,
78300 Poissy, France
Tel: +33 (0)1 39 65 01 06

***Interim Art/Maureen Paley***
21 Herald Street, London
E2 6JT, UK
Tel: +44 (0)20 7729 4112
Fax: +44 (0)20 7729 4113
High-end contemporary art.

***Musée des Arts Décoratifs***
107 rue de Rivoli,
75001 Paris, France
Tel: +33 (0)1 44 55 57 50

***Musée des Arts Décoratifs de Montreal***
2929 rue Jeanne d'Arc,
Montreal, Quebec H1W 3W2,
Canada
Tel: +1 514 259 2575

***Museu de les Arts Decoratives***
Palau Reial de Pedralbes,
Avenida Diagonal 686,
08034 Barcelona, Spain
Tel: +34 (0)3 280 50 24

***Museum of Fine Arts***
465 Huntington Avenue,
Boston, MA 02115, USA
Tel: +1 617 267 9300

***Museum of Modern Art***
11 West 53rd Street,
New York, NY10019, USA
Tel: +1 212 708 9480

***Parsons School of Design***
66 Fifth Avenue, New York,
NY 10011, USA
Tel: +1 212 229 8900

***Philadelphia Museum of Art***
26th Street & Benjamin
Franklin Parkway,
Philadelphia, PA 19130, USA
Tel: +1 215 763 8100

***Saarinen/Cranbrook Academy of Art***
1221 North Woodward,
Bloomfield Hills,
MI 48304-2824, USA
Tel: +1 248 645 3300

***White Cube 2***
48 Hoxton Square, London
N1 6PB, UK
Tel: +44 (0)20 7930 5373
www.whitecube.com
Contemporary art gallery.

## WEBSITE SOURCES

***Anthony Gallo Acoustics***
Tel: +44 (0)1555 666444
www.anthonygallo.co.uk
Decorative acoustic speakers.

***Art Antique Merchants e-Bay Auctions***
www.artmerch.com

***ClassicOnline - Modern Furniture***
www.classiconline.com

***Past Present Future Home***
pastpresentfuture.net

## INTERIOR DESIGNERS AND ARCHITECTS

***Maxime d'Angeac Architecte***
41 rue Puchet, 75017 Paris, France
Tel: +33 (0)1 53 11 01 82
dangeac@club-internet.fr
Appears on pages 138 (above right), 201.

***Asfour Guzy***
594 Broadway, Suite 1204, New York, NY 10012, USA
Tel: +1 212 334 9350
www.asfourguzy.com

***Tristan Auer***
5a cour de la Métaine, 75020 Paris, France
Tel/Fax: +33 (0)1 43 49 57 20
Appears on pages 138 (above right), 201.

***John Barman Inc.***
500 Park Avenue, Suite 21a, New York, NY 10022, USA
Tel: +1 212 838 9443
Fax: +1 212 838 4028
www.johnbarman.com
Appears on pages 28–31.

***Solis Betancourt***
1739 Connecticut Avenue NW, Washington, DC 20009, USA
Tel: +1 202 659 8734
www.solisbetancourt.com

***Bruce Bierman Design Inc.***
29th West 15th Street, New York, NY 10011, USA
Tel: +1 212 243 1935
Fax: +1 212 243 6615
www.biermandesign.com
Appears on back jacket and pages 163, 170, 180.

***Laurent Buttazzoni***
62 rue de Montreuil, 75011 Paris, France
Tel: +33 (0)1 40 09 98 49
Appears on pages 64–7, 151, 195.

***Leonardo Chalupowicz***
3527 Landa Street, Los Angeles, CA 90039, USA
Tel: +1 323 660 8261
Fax: +1 323 843 9828
www.chalupowicz.com
Appears on pages 42–3, 62–3, 109, 120 (below right), 127, 145, 155, 176 (above), 181 (below right).

***Fred Collin***
Flat 5-6, 30 Cleveland Square, London W2 6DD, UK
Tel: +44 (0)20 7262 1956
Fax: +44 (0)870 922 3299
Appears on pages 147, 182 (above).

***Jamie Drake Associates***
315 East 62nd Street, 5th Floor, New York, NY 10021, USA
Tel: +1 212 754 3099
www.drakedesignassociates.com
Appears on pages 111 (above right), 200 (above right), 209 (above).

***Atelier d'Architecture M Frisenna SCPL***
15 rue de Verviers, 4020 Liège, Belgium
Tel: +32 (0)4 341 5786
Appears on pages 11, 161.

***Fusion Design & Architecture***
4 Risborough Street, London SE1 0HE, UK
Tel: +44 (0)20 7928 9982
www.fusiondna.co.uk

***Eric Gizard Associates***
14 rue Crespin du Cast, 75011 Paris, France
Tel: +33 (0)1 55 28 38 58
www.gizardassocies.com, information@gizardassocies.com
Appears on pages 6, 12–13, 32–3, 54–5, 96–7, 103 (above left), 106 (above left), 113 (below), 122, 133, 136 (above), 164, 178 (above).

***Alexander Gorlin Architect***
137 Varick Street, 5th Floor, New York, NY 10013, USA
Tel: +1 212 229 1199
Fax: +1 212 206 3590
www.gorlinarchitect.com

***Hudson Architects***
49-59 Old Street, London EC1V 9HX, UK
Tel: +44 (0)20 7490 3411
Fax +44 (0)20 7490 3412
www.hudsonarchitects.co.uk
Appears on pages 116, 137 (above & below left), 157 (right).

***Les Editions Dominique Kieffer*** (fabric designer)
8 rue Herold, 75001 Paris, France
Tel: +33 (0)1 42 21 32 44
www.dkieffer.com
Appears on pages 110, 203 (below left), 208 (below left & right).

***Kold – Karl Fournier & Olivier Marty***
7 rue Geoffroy l'Angevin, 75004 Paris, France
Tel: +33 (0)1 42 71 13 92
F: +33 (0)1 42 71 13 94
kold@noos.fr
Appears on pages 74–5, 152, 194 (above).

***François Marcq***
8 rue Fernand Neuray, 1050 Brussels, Belgium
Tel: +32 (0)2 513 1328
Francoismarcq@skynet.be
Appears on pages 86–9.

***Audrey Matlock Architects***
88 West Broadway, New York, NY 10007, USA
Tel: +1 212 267 2378
Fax: +1 212 267 6850
www.audreymatlockarchitect.com
Appears on pages 174–5, 181 (below left), 196 (below).

***Frédéric Méchiche***
14 rue Saint Croix de la Bretonnerie, 75004 Paris, France
Tel : +33 (0)1 42 78 78 28
Fax: +33 (0)1 42 78 23 30
Appears on pages 84–5, 129 (below), 176 (below).

***Laurence Pichon-Kriegel***
loladesign2002@yahoo.com
Appears on pages 134 (below right), 177.

***Kristiina Ratia***
USA
Tel: +1 203 852 0027
Kristiinaratia@aol.com
Appears on pages 40–1, 112 (below left).

***Rios Associates Inc.***
8008 West 3rd Street, Los Angeles, CA 90048, USA
Tel: +1 323 634 9220
Mark@rios.com
Appears on pages 46–9, 101–2, 121, 130, 139, 175 (above left & right), 190 (below), 209 (below left).

***Stephen Roberts Inc.***
Fourth Floor, 250 West Broadway, New York, NY 10013, USA
Tel: +1 212 966 6930 or +1 917 626 7401
www.stephenroberts.com, robertsnyc@aol.com
Appears on pages 4–5, 117 (below), 135 (below), 138 (below), 148, 156, 182–3.

***Shelton, Mindel & Associates***
143 West 20th Street, New York, NY 10011, USA
Tel: +1 212 243 3939
Fax: +1 212 2727 7310
Appears on pages 24–7, 123 (above right), 146 (above right), 189, 190 (above).

***Stedila Design Inc.***
135 East 53rd Street, New York, NY 10022, USA
Tel: +1 212 751 4281
Fax: +1 212 751 6698
john@stediladesign.com
Appears on pages 70–1.

***Seth Stein Architects***
15 Grand Union Centre, West Row, London W10 5AS, UK
Tel: +44 (0)20 8968 8581
www.sethstein.com

***Vincent Van Duysen***
Lombardenvest 34, 2000 Antwerp, Belgium
Tel: +32 (0)3 205 9190
Fax: +32 (0)3 204 0138
www.vanduysen.be
Appears on front jacket and pages 36–7, 52–3, 90–1, 115, 132 (below), 153 (above), 202, 207.

***Jean-Marc Vynckier***
A Propos de Lieu, 49 rue Daubenton, 59100 Roubaix, France
Tel: +33 (0)3 20 27 86 59
Appears on pages 9 (below), 80 (left & centre), 80–3, 123 (above left), 166 (above right), 167 (all pictures), 171 (below right), 184–5, 192.

***Jocelyn Warner***
19-20 Sunbury Workshop, Swanfield Street, London E2 7LF, UK
Tel: +44 (0)207 613 4773
jocelyn@jocelynwarner.com
Appears on pages 112 (above & below right), 113 (above).

***Wells Mackereth Architects***
Unit 14, Archer Street Studios, 10-11 Archer Street, London W1D 7AZ, UK
Tel: +44 (0)20 7287 5504
www.wellsmackereth.com, hq@wellsmackereth.com
Appears on pages 72–3.

***Vicente Wolf Associates Inc.***
333 West 39th Street, 10th Floor, New York, NY 10018, USA
Tel: +1 212 465 0590
Fax: +1 212 465 0639
Appears on pages 16–19, 128, 200 (below right), 210.

***Michael Wolfson Architect***
15 Cardinal Mansions, Carlisle Place, London SW1P 1EY, UK
Tel: +44 (0)20 7630 9377
www.wolfsondesign.com
Appears on pages 58–61.

***1100 Architect***
435 Hudson Street, New York, NY 10014, USA
Tel: +1 212 645 1011
Fax: +1 212 645 4670
www.1100architect.com
Appears on pages 38–9.

# INDEX


"absence of style" design movement, 38
accessories, 187
Addison, Joseph, 187
Adilon Courtrai, 83
Adnet, Jacques, 169
Aestus radiators, 160, 161
Ando, Tadao, 104
"Anglepoise" lamps, 170
Anti Form, 45
architectonics, 26
Arets, Wiel, 86
armchairs, 194–7
club, 196
"The Egg", 197
Art Deco
living room, 28–31
windows, 136
art and ornament, 206–11
fixed pieces, 208–9
groups of pictures, 206
movable pieces, 209–10
Arts and Crafts
chairs 190
lamps 24
tables 26, 190
Australian aborigines, and fire, 154

Badgley, Mark, 110
bare facts kitchen, 52–3
bare walls, 104–5
Barker, Katy, 64, 66
Barman, John, 28, 29, 30
basins, 94, 148–51
double, 149, 150
glass, 146
bathrooms, 79–92
basins, 94, 146, 148–51
conversations in, 149
dividers between bedrooms and, 81
doors, 134
elevated space, 80–3
flooring, 94
materials in, 79, 94
mirrors, 79, 84, 85, 88, 90
modern marble, 84–5
seamless, 90–1
solidity, 92–5
storage, 79, 173
taps, 85, 88, 91, 94
tiles, 108, 109
urban logic, 86–9
walls, 102, 107
windows, 137
see also showers
baths, 79, 91, 92, 93, 146–7
Japanese hot tubs, 146
Bauhaus door handles, 130
Bauhaus lamps, 167
beams, 140, 141
Beaux-Arts, 125
bedrooms, 69–76
beds, 69, 70, 72, 77
calm neutrality, 76–7
cushions, 205
dividers between bathrooms and, 81
exposed, 74–5
fireplaces, 158
generosity in, 69
private view, 70–1
simplicity, 72–3
wall cladding in, 106
Berkel, Ben Van, 86
Berlin, New Art Gallery, 106
Bierman, Bruce, 148
black walls, 110, 111
blinds, 201, 202
Boesch, Elisabeth, 106
Boesch, Martin, 106
Boffi bathroom furnishings, 92, 93
bookcases, 22, 23, 197
books, storage, 173, 176
Botta, Maria, 104
Boulder Thorgusson, Bob, 42–3
Boyd, Ann, 50, 76
brick walls, 100, 104
Brittany, 143
Abbaye de Boquen, 91
Brown, Capability, 25
Bruce Bierman Design, 170
Brutalism, 89
Bulthaup, 181
bungalows, 125
Buttazzoni, Laurent, 66, 148, 195

Cabinets, built-in, 175
calm neutrality bedroom, 76–7
Carmelite nuns, 90, 91
carpentry, 118
carpets, 114, 122–3
Carrara marble
bathrooms, 84, 85, 91, 151
in dining rooms, 36
sinks, 152
tiles, 108
central access, connecting spaces, 62–3
ceramic tiles, 108
chairs 190–3
bent metal tubing 193
brown upholstered 31
comfortable 190, 191
"Costes" chair 192, 193
foam rubber 190
high-backed 188
Nigerian leather 24
Vincente Wolf style 16, 17
Chalupowicz, Leonardo, 42, 62
cherry wood floors, 118, 119
Chesterton, G.K., *Tremendous Trifles*, 69
chipboard floors, 117
circular tables, 193
cladding, interior wood, 26, 106–7
Clinton era, 89
closets, 79, 178–9
clothes storage, 178–9
Codman, Ogden, Jr, 125
Colleoni, Susanna, 20, 21–3, 92–5
Collin, Fred, 147, 182
colour, 187
kitchens, 54–5
and light, 162
living rooms, 28–31
tables and chairs, 189
walls, 110–11
columns, 141
comfort
comfort living room, 16–19
comfortable chairs, 190, 191
comfortable sofas, 194–7
composite floors, 116–17
computer imaging, and floorplans, 188
concrete walls, 100, 104
connecting spaces, 57–67
central access, 62–3
hallways, 57
linking rooms, 64–7
openness, 58–61
options for, 57
and pathology, 57
staircases, 57
Conran, Jasper, 9, 45, 50–1, 76–7
bathroom, 107
oak floor, 119
Corbiau, Marc, 36
Corbusier, Le, see Le Corbusier
"Costes" chair, 192, 193
Coward, Noël, 188
Cranfield, Frances, 197
Crawshaw, Richard, 79
Cretan mosaics, 114
curtains, 200–3
cushions, 204–5
CVO Fireplaces, 156, 158–9

dark walls, 110
David B. Gamble house (California), 106
De Stijl group, 46
Delcourt, Christophe, 169
desk lamps, 165
Dickinson, Emily, 173
dining rooms, 35–42
flowing space, 38–9
indoor outdoor, 36–7
storage, 174
tables and chairs, 190–3
tonal, 40–1
transparency, 42–3
doors, 125, 128, 130–2
Bauhaus handles, 130
changing door proportions, 135
double, 131
glass, 132, 133, 134
oak, 26
sliding, 130, 132
steel-framed, 131, 135
stone, 132
wooden, 132*f*3
downsizing, 89
Drake, Jamie, 209
Dunning, Brad, 26
"Duplex" lamp, 170
Duravit, 88

Eames, Charles and Ray, 197
Ecart International, 170
Edinburgh Castle, 106
Edison, Thomas, 162
Egyptian doors, 131–2
1100 Architect, 38, 180
electricity, 143
cables, 15
electrical sockets, 79
elemental kitchen, 46–9
elevated space bathroom, 80–3
elevators, 125
epoxy resin, 117
Everett, Rupert, 135
exposed bedroom, 74–5

fabric, 198
Farnsworth House, 8, 99
Fassina, Giancarlo, 170
fire, 154, 156–9
fireplaces, 22, 32, 33
CVO "Firebowl", 159
marble, 156
"Ripple", 158
traditional, 159
Victorian surrounds, 157
floating walls, 102
floors, 114–23
bathrooms, 94
carpets, 114, 122–3
composite, 116–17
marble, 114, 117
mosaic, 114
rugs, 29, 31, 114, 122–3
sanding and sealing, 118–19
seamless flooring, 116
stone, 114, 120–1
terrazzo, 114, 117, 121
white, 21
wooden, 114, 118–19
flowing space dining room, 38–9
fluorescent lights, 166
foam-rubber chairs, 190
Foster, Sir Norman, 61
Fournier, Karl, 74
France, food and dining in, 35
Frank, Jean Michel, 194
Franke sinks, 152, 153
Frisenna, Marina, 160
furniture, 188–97
as accessories, 187
Art Deco, 28–30
chairs, 190–3
floorplans, 188
geometric living room, 32
high chairbacks, 188
overscale, 188
and "roomscape", 188
Shaker, 190
sofas and armchairs, 194–7
storage units, 175–6

tables, 190–3

gas fires, 156
gateleg tables, 190

geometry living room, 32–3
gifts, 187
Gill, David, 45
Gizard, Eric, 32–3, 45, 54–5, 107, 113, 122, 135
glass
basins, 146
brick, 108
as a building material, 136
doors, 132, 133, 134
tiles, 108
walls, 100, 102
Glass House (Connecticut), 99
Goebal, Heinrich, 169
Gorlin, Alexander, 30
Graham, Kelly, 30
Greek *klismos* form, 39
Green Gallery, New York, 45
Greer, Michael, *Inside Design*, 201–2
Gropius, Walter, 130, 135
Guedroitz, Prince Nicholas, 58

hallways, 57
Ham House, Surrey, 194
Harding, Martin, 175
heat, 143, 154–61
fire, 154, 156–9
living rooms, 15
radiators, 160–1
wood-burning stoves, 157, 158
Henningsen, Fritz, 26
Henningsen, Poul, 164, 165, 168
Hepplewhite furniture, 188
Heraclitus, 61
Hesse, Eva, 45
Hicks, David, 123
Higgins, Gregory, 39
high-backed chairs, 188
Hilmer & Sattler, 106
Hirst, Damien, 136
Holland, furniture in, 194
Horace, *Odes*, 10
Hudson, Anthony, 8, 104, 140
humidifiers, 160

illusion, 15
indoor outdoor dining room, 36–7

Jacobsen, Arne, 64, 148, 197
Japan
sliding shoji screens, 103, 135
*tatami* mats, 122, 123
Jiricna, Eva, 126
Johnson, Philip, 99, 136
Judd, Donald, 193
Juicy Couture, 42

Keller, A.G., 156
Kieffer, Dominique, 202, 209
kirkstone, 120
kitchens, 45–55
bare facts, 52–3
cookers and hobs, 180
countertops, 182
elemental, 46–9
lighting, 165
and Minimalism, 45, 52, 53
personal colour, 54–5
sinks, 152–3
soft Modernism, 50–1
storage, 173, 180–4
Klint, Kaare, 24
Knole, Kent, 197
Kold (architecture and design company), 74

lamps, 165, 168–71
"Anglepoise", 170
Arts and Crafts, 24
"Duplex", 171
"framed", 168, 169
Henningsen, 165
pairs of, 166
"Tolomeo", 171
vintage task lamps, 170
lampshades, 165
Larkin, Philip, 135
Laverière, Jeannette, 132
LCD (Liquid Crystal Display) glass, 136
Le Corbusier, 10, 57, 80, 135
*Vers une architecture*, 10
Lehrecke, Chris, 169
lights and lighting, 143, 162–71, 187
bathrooms, 88
ceiling spots, 167
dining tables, 20
downlighters, 167
fluorescent, 166
kitchens, 165
living rooms, 15
Murano-glass, 164
natural, 167
white light living room, 20–3
uplighters, 165
see also lamps
limestone basins, 148
linking rooms, 64–7
lintel beams, 141
living rooms, 15–33
colour, 28–31
comfort, 16–19
cushions, 204, 205
dining areas in, 22
flooring, 117
geometry, 32–3
heating, 15
lighting, 15
materials, 15
open-plan, 15, 30
saving space, 15
sofas and armchairs, 194–7
storage, 175–6
surfaces, 15
texture, 24–7
white light, 20–3
Lloyd Wright, Frank, 135
London
Architectural Association, 58
British Museum, 132
Chelsea Paint Library, 76
St Martin's School of Art, 76
Waterloo Bridge, 7
Loos, Adolf, 106
Louis XI, King of France, 113
Lucchi, Michele de, 164, 170

Mackereth, Sally, 72–3
McKim, Charles, 125
marble
cladding, 106
fireplaces, 156
floors, 114
see also Carrara marble
Marcq, François, 86, 89
Marimmekko (Finnish textile company), 41
Marty, Olivier, 74
Matlock, Audrey, 197
Méchiche, Frédéric, 84–5, 118, 169
metal beams, 140
metal cladding, 106
methacrylate resin, 117
Mies van der Rohe, Ludwig, 8, 99, 135–6
Mindel, Lee, 122
Minimalism, 89
and kitchens, 45, 52, 53
staircases, 58, 61
Minotti kitchens, 181
mirrored tiles, 108
mirrors, 210, 211
in bathrooms, 79, 84, 85, 88, 90
Mischka, James, 110
modern marble bathroom, 84–5
Modernism, 89, 99, 129, 136, 138
Mondrian, Piet, 46
Mongiardino, Renzo, 10
Morris, Robert, 45, 53
mosaics, 108, 114
Mouille, Serge, 164
Myson towel warmers, 161

Nakamura, Toshio, 100
Nakashima, George, 25
Neutra, Richard, 46, 136
Nicholson, Ben, 53
Nigerian leather chair, 24

oak
in dining rooms, 36
doors, 26
floors, 118, 119
German white rift oak, 25, 26, 118
panelling, 106, 107
open-plan living, 8, 15, 30, 54, 62–3
Osiris, 129

painted wooden floors, 119
Papua New Guinea, 154
Paris Rive Gauche, 33
parquet floors, 118, 119
pathology, and connecting spaces, 57
Pawson, John, 117
Pepys, Samuel, 197
Peretti, Elsa, 30
Picasso, Pablo, 206
pilasters, 141
Piscuskas, David, 38
plaster cladding, 106
Platonic Fireplace Company, 159
plywood, 106
plywood chairs, 193
Poliform, 106
Ponti, Gio, 30
Portland stone, 7, 159
Post Minimalism, 45
Poulsen, Louis, 164
Prague, Villa Muller, 106
Pre-Raphaelites, 198
private view bedroom, 70–1
Process Art, 45
Prometheus, 156
Proust, Marcel, 91
Pucci, Ralph, 16, 169
Putman, Andrée, 81, 170, 188

Quaker Barn, 104

radiators, 160–1
Ratia, Kristiina, 40–1
resin baths, 147
resin floors, 117
Rhinebeck "farm" (upstate New York) 24–7
Rieber's "water station", 153
Riehm, Juergen, 38
Rietfeld, Gerrit, 46
Rios, Mark, 45, 46–9, 107, 130, 138, 209
Risom, Jens, 110
Roberts, Stephen, 130, 183
Robuchon, Joël, 84
Rogers, Richard, 126
Roman blinds, 201, 202
Roman mosaics, 108
RSJs (reinforced steel joists), 100
rugs, 114, 122–3
Ruskin, John, 198

Saarinen, Eero, 126
SAD (Seasonal Affective Disorder), 162
Sander, Jil, 106
Scholtes, Pierre, 113
sconces, 169
seamless bathroom, 90–1
seamless flooring, 116
Serra, Richard, 45
Shakers, 190
Sheldon, Mindel & Associates, 25–6
Shelton and Mindel, 107, 197
shelves, 176, 177, 211
Sheridan, Richard, *The Critic*, 21
showers, 82, 83, 84, 95, 144
domes, 144
power showers, 144
pull-out, 147
Venturi, 144
shutters, 136, 137, 138, 202
SieMatic sinks, 152
simplicity bedroom, 72–3
sinks, 152–3
Skaist Levy, Pam, 9, 42, 62–3
slate floors, 120
slate tiles, 109
sliding doors, 130, 132
sliding shoji screens, 103, 135
Smallbone, 181
Smallwood, Christopher, 123
Soane, Sir John, 167
sofas, 194–7
origins of the word "sofa", 204
soft furnishings, 198–205
cushions, 204–5
window treatments, 200–3
soft Modernist kitchen, 50–1
solar power, 143
solidity bathroom, 92–5
*The Spectator*, 187
spotlights, 167
stained floors, 119
stainless steel sinks, 153
staircases, 57, 126–9
cantilevered, 126
concrete, 126
and exposed walls, 104
freestanding, 127
glass, 126
industrial-style, 129
legal requirements, 126
Minimalist, 58, 61
single-flight, 129
spiral, 126
steel, 126, 129
tops of, 129
traditional, 128
wooden, 126, 129

Starck, Philippe, 80, 88, 193
  "Costes" chair, 192, 193
Stedila, John, 9, 70–1, 110
steel supports, 140
Stein, Gertrude, 173
Stockholm, Skokloster Palace, 194
stone
  bathroom basins, 150
  cladding, 106
  doors, 132
  floors, 114, 120–1
  tiles, 108, 109
  walls, 104
storage, 173–81
  bathrooms, 79, 173
  books, 173
  clothing, 178–9
  kitchens, 173, 180–4
  leisure items, 175–6
striped wallpaper, 112
structure, 125–41, 187
  and computer-aided imaging, 125
  doors, 125, 128, 130–2
  elements, 140–1
  windows, 125, 128, 134–9
  see also staircases
Sumner, W.G., 156
surfaces, 9, 99–123
  living rooms, 15
  and the value of illusion, 15
  see also floors; walls
Switzerland, Felsen-Therme spa, 94

**t**ables, 190–3
  circular, 193
  gateleg tables, 190
  metal-based, 30
  table legs, 190
  "Tulip" table, 190
  Vincente Wolf style, 16, 18
taps
  bathrooms, 85, 88, 91, 94
  sinks, 153
*tatami* mats, 122, 123
televisions, 173, 175
Tennyson, Alfred, Lord, 35
terrazzo floors, 114, 117, 121
textures
  tables and chairs, 189
  texture living room, 24–7
Tiffany 30
tiles, 108–9
"Tolomeo" lamp, 171
Tolstoy, Leo, *War and Peace*, 57
tonal dining room, 40–1
Torke, Michael, 57
towel rails, 160, 161
transparency dining room, 42–3
travertine cladding, 106
Tremlett, David, 113
Tsunami, 181
"Tulip" table, 190

**u**rban logic bathroom, 86–9

**V**an, see Edric van Vredenburgh
Van Duysen, Vincent, 9, 36–7, 45, 52–3, 194, 202
  fireplace, 158, 159
  rectangular sinks, 152
  seamless flooring, 116
  seamlessness bathroom, 90–1
Van Outersterp, Christian and Carolyn, 157
vintage task lamps, 170
Virgil, 35
Vogal, Julian, 73
volcanic stones, 120
Volevatch, 147
Vredenburgh, Edric van, 211
Vynckier, Jean-Marc, 80

**w**allpaper, 112–13
walls, 100–13
  bare, 104–5
  brick, 100, 104
  colour, 110–11
  concrete, 100, 104
  floating, 102
  glass, 100, 102
  inserting, 102–3
  patterns, 112–13
  removing internal walls, 100
  stone, 104
  tiles, 108–9
  white, 21
  wooden, 26, 100, 106–7
Warner, Jocelyn, 113
water, 143, 144–53
  basins, 146, 148–51
  baths, 79, 91, 92, 93, 146–7
  showers, 82, 83, 84, 95, 144
  sinks, 152–3
Weeks, David, 164, 169
Wells, James, 73
Wells Mackereth, 73
Werner, Bettina, 16
wet rooms, 148, 160
Wharton, Edith, *The Decoration of Houses*, 125
white light living room, 20–3
White, Stanford, 125
Wigmore, John, 169
Wilde, Oscar, 125
windows, 125, 128, 134–9
  bathrooms, 137
  curtains and blinds, 200–3
  floor-to-ceiling, 139
  interior, 138
  portholes, 137
  shutters, 136, 137, 138, 202
  sliding shoji screens, 134
  in Victorian times, 135
  "window wall" houses, 135–6
Wolf, Vicente, 16–17, 18
Wolfson, Michael, 58–61, 141
wood
  in bathrooms, 79, 94
  beams, 140
  doors, 132–3
  floors, 114, 118–19
    geometric pattern on, 118
    painted, 119
  German white rift oak, 25, 26, 118
  walls, 100
    cladding, 26, 106–7
wood-burning stoves, 157, 158
World War II, 7
Wrangel, Carl Gustaf, 194

# Picture location credits

Front jacket: an apartment in Brussels designed by Vincent Van Duysen
Back jacket: Penthouse loft in New York designed by Bruce Bierman Design Inc.
Pages 1, 44 left, 50–51, 68 centre, 76–77, 107 below, 119 left, 136 below, 203 above left, Jasper Conran's home in London; pages 2, 6, 12–13, 14 right, 32–33, 96–97, 103 above left, 113 below, 133, 135 above, 146 above left, 164, 175 below, Peter Wheeler and Pascale Revert's London home, designed by Eric Gizard; pages 4–5, 103 below right, 117 below, 131 below, 135 below, 138 below, 148, 156, 182–183, James Gager & Richard Ferretti's New York apartment, designed by Stephen Roberts; pages 9 above, 34 left, 38–39, 123 below, 132 above, 149 above, 172 centre, 180, Keith and Cathy Abell's New York house, designed by 1100 Architect; pages 9 below, 78 left & centre, 80–83, 123 above left, 166 above right, 167, 171 below right, 184–185, 192, Jean-Marc Vynckier's home in Lille; pages 11, 104 left & above right, 108 below right, 120 above right, 129 above right, 140 right, 141 far left, 160 above, 161, 179 above left, Mr & Mrs Boucquiau's house in Belgium, designed by Marina Frisenna; pages 14 left & centre, 24–27, 98 centre, 107 above right, 118 far left, 123 above right, 146 above right, 165 above left, 168 below, 169 below, 189, 190 above, 196 above left, 197 right, a house in New York designed by Shelton, Mindel & Associates; pages 16–19, 128, 169 above left, 200 below right, 210, 211 below right, Ralph and Ann Pucci's New York home, furnished in collaboration with Vicente Wolf; pages 20–23, 92–95, 103 below left, 117 above, 131 above left, 134 above right, 142 left, 150 below, 172 left, 181 above, 182 below, 186 right, 191, Susanna Colleoni & Didi Huber's home in Milan; pages 28–31, 205 below left, an apartment in New York designed by John Barman Inc.; pages 34 centre, 36–37, 44 centre, 52–53, 90–91, 106 below right, 115, 131 above right, 132 below, 153 above, 159 above left, 160 below left, 194 below, 197 left, 202, 207, an apartment in Brussels designed by Vincent Van Duysen; pages 34 right, 42–43, 56 centre, 62–63, 103 above right, 109, 120 below right, 127, 134 above left, 138 above left, 145, 155, 176 above, 181 below right, 209 below right, Pam Skaist Levy's Hollywood Hills house, designed by Leonardo Chalupowicz; pages 40–41, 112 below left, 159 above right, Kristiina Ratia's Connecticut home; pages 44 right, 46–49, 98 right, 101–102, 106 above right, 108 above, 121, 124 left & centre, 130, 139, 175 above left & right, 190 below, 209 below left, Mark Rios's home in Los Angeles; pages 54–55, 106 above left, 122, 134 below left, 136 above, 146 below, 153 below, 166 above left, 178 above, Eric Gizard's apartment in Paris; pages 56 left, 58–61, 141 far right, 204 left, a house in London designed by Michael Wolfson Architect; pages 56 right, 64–67, 149 below left, 151, 193 below, 195, 203 right, Katy Barker's Paris apartment, designed by Laurent Buttazzoni; pages 68 left, 70–71, 111 above left, 160 below right, John Stedila's house in the Hamptons; pages 68 right, 72–73, 143 left, 142 centre & above right, 211 above, Sally Mackereth & Julian Vogel's house in London, designed by Wells Mackereth; pages 74–75, 107 above left, 152, 186 left, 193 above left, 194 above, 199, an apartment in Paris designed by Kold; pages 78 right, 84–85, 108 below left, 118 right, 129 below, 168 above left, 176 below, 200 left, an apartment in Paris designed by Frédéric Méchiché; pages 86–89, 118 far right, 172 right, 179 below left, an apartment in Belgium designed by François Marcq; pages 98 left, 104 below right, 116, 137 above & below left, 140 far left & far right, 141 right, 142 right, 157 right, 158 below right, Anthony Hudson's barn in Norfolk; pages 105, 118 left, 124 right, 126 left, 137 below right, Maxime & Athénais d'Angeac's home in Paris; pages 110, 119 far left, 203 below left, 204 below, 205 above left & right, 208 below, Dominique Kieffer's apartment in Paris; pages 111 above right, 186 centre, 200 above right, 209 above, Jamie Drake's apartment in New York; pages 111 below, 169 above right, 196 above right, Mark Badgley and James Mischka's New York apartment; pages 112 above and below right, 113 above, Jocelyn & Simon Warner's house in London; page 119 right, Deirdre Dyson's home in London; pages 119 far right, 138 above right, 201, Tristan Auer's apartment in Paris; pages 120 above left, 126 right, a house in the Hamptons designed by Solis Betancourt; pages 120 below left, 157 left, 158 above & below left, 159 below, 171 above left, 178 below, 179 above right, 208 above, the home of Carolyn & Christian van Outersterp of CVO Fireplaces in the northeast of England; pages 129 above left, 166 below right, Sophie Douglas of Fusion Design & Architecture's converted barn in Somerset; pages 134 below right, 168 above right, 171 above right, 177, 211 below left, Laurence Kriegel's apartment in New York; page 140 left, Sara & Joe Farley's apartment in New York, designed by Asfour Guzy; pages 147, 179 below right, 182 above, 193 above right, 205 below right, Fred & Helen Collin's house in London; pages 149 below right, 163, 166 below left, 170, 171 below left, a penthouse loft in New York designed by Bruce Bierman Design Inc.; page 150 above left, Richard & Lucille Lewin's house in London, designed by Seth Stein; page 165 below, Suzanne Tick & Terry Mowers's apartment in New York; pages 174–175, 181 below left, 196 below, Martin Harding's house, designed by Audrey Matlock.
Front endpaper: 1& 7) Mark Rios's home in Los Angeles; 2) Anthony Hudson's barn in Norfolk; 3) Peter Wheeler & Pascale Revert's London home, designed by Eric Gizard; 4 & 6) centre a house in New York designed by Shelton, Mindel and Associates; 5) an apartment in Belgium designed by François Marcq; 8) an apartment in Brussels designed by Vincent Van Duysen.
Back endpaper: 1) Maxime & Athénais d'Angeac's home in Paris; 2) Anthony Hudson's barn in Norfolk; 3) an apartment in Paris designed by Kold; 4) an apartment in Paris designed by Frédéric Méchiche; 5) an apartment in Brussels designed by Vincent Van Duysen; 6) Mark Rios's home in Los Angeles; 7) Jamie Drake's apartment in New York; 8) Keith & Cathy Abell's New York house, designed by 1100 Architect.

# ACKNOWLEDGMENTS

The author would like to thank all who participated in the making of this book: the architects, designers and skilled workers in the many disciplines covered, and particulary the home owners, whose lives we disrupt, just briefly, but enough to matter.

Thanks are also due to the usual and unbending familial support, to Paul of course, the boys, Miles and Edwin, for their understanding, and to friends whose boundless enthusiasm never seems to falter.

Thank you, too, to Jacqui Small and her publishing team for their professionalism at every turn, to Lawrence Morton for his artistry, and to the dear Andrew Wood, who made it seem all so easy.